BE STILL

Designing and Leading Contemplative Retreats

Jane E. Vennard

An Alban Institute Book
ROWMAN & LITTLEFIELD
Lanham • Boulder • New York • Toronto • Plymouth, UK

First Rowman & Littlefield paperback edition 2014

Published by Rowman & Littlefield
4501 Forbes Blvd, Suite 200, Lanham, MD 20706
www.rowman.com

10 Thornbury Road, Plymouth PL6 7PP, United Kingdom

Library of Congress Cataloging Card Number 99-69584

ISBN 13: 978-1-56699-229-9 (pbk: alk. paper)

⊖™ The paper used in this publication meets the minimum requirements of American National Standard for Information Sciences—Permanence of Paper for Printed Library Materials, ANSI/NISO Z39.48-1992.

Printed in the United States of America

For all those with whom
I have shared
sacred moments of stillness.

Be still and know that I am God.

Psalm 46:10

CONTENTS

PREFACE

R etreats have been part of my life for as long as I can remember. As a child, I loved to ride my bicycle around the streets of town going nowhere. I would feel the wind in my hair, see the roads open before me, hear the voices of people recede as I sped by. I felt joy and delight in my freedom. Later I discovered the Children's Library, which had a garden for quiet reading. I would go there to spend the afternoon, alternately devouring books and lying on my back watching the clouds.

Retreating was harder as a teenager. The pressure to be social and active made my longing for solitude and silence seem odd. I would go to my room ostensibly to do homework, but I would simply sit doing nothing, feeling great peace along with twinges of guilt.

In my young adult years, I began to write poems. I wandered city streets, mountain trails, and the halls of the schools in which I taught, looking for material that touched my heart in ways that could only be responded to in poetry. The practice of writing served me well as my marriage began to disintegrate. In my despair and pain, I would go off alone, trying to find meaning in the chaos. The only order I found was in the written word.

When my marriage ended, I took solitary backpacking trips with my dog, Emily. I opened myself to the healing power of the woods, the mountains, the streams, and the rocks. The sounds of crickets and bird song, the sight of a hawk drifting on the air currents, the glimpse of a white fox all served to bring my soul to rest.

During that time I also discovered intentional retreats, with leaders and participants and themes and activities and discussions all planned to guide us inward, open us to new possibilities, teach us new ways of being in the world. When I went to seminary, I found the wonder of silent retreat houses (usually Roman Catholic) with a ministry of hospitality. They provided food and shelter, community prayers and spiritual direction. They welcomed tears and laughter, despair and delight, and the company of other retreatants whom I felt I knew, although we never exchanged a word.

When I remarried and was blessed with two stepsons, my younger was confused about my going off by myself. "Why are you going?" he would ask. "When will you come back? Can I go? I'll be *real* quiet. I promise. *Please. Let me go too!*" How do you explain to a seven-year-old that as much as you love him, you need to be alone? How do you reassure him that you will be back? How do you articulate the longing that would rise up within me to shift my attention for only a few days away from daily life to God? I never found the words, but he seemed comforted when I told him that I would not let his father come with me either. He said in great relief, "I thought Daddy wasn't going because he has to take care of us." Over years both boys came to understand that "going off alone" was just what I did. I think they also realized that I always came back with more love to give.

Retreat Ministry

After graduation and ordination I began my ministry of teaching and spiritual direction. I found in many of my students and directees the same longing for silence that I experienced. Some were familiar with retreats, but most had no idea how to respond to their inner promptings in any way other than grabbing a moment here and there within their busy lives. When I offered the idea of a retreat, they were excited but also afraid. "Where will I go?" "What will I do?" "How can I explain this to my family?" "Isn't it selfish?" "What if I hate it?"

I offered some suggestions, we worked through issues, we prayed about it, and many directees took the risk either to go off alone, spend time at a retreat house, or find a way to have intentional retreat time at home. They all had different experiences, and those who went on more than one or two retreats discovered that each time, their experience would vary. But all of them reported a significant movement in their spiritual lives as a result of their retreat experiences.

Because seminary students are overwhelmed with study and internships, community activities, jobs, and families, most of them could find no way to experience retreats. To meet their need for quiet, I designed a retreat class during winter interterm at the Iliff School of Theology, where I am senior adjunct faculty in prayer and spirituality. This retreat is held from Monday to Friday at the nearby Sacred Heart Jesuit Retreat House. The students receive academic credit, although there are no papers or grades, little traditional instruction, and a lot of silence. The students report a renewal of their faith, clarification of their call to ministry, and an experience of community that they do not find on campus.

I also offer a shorter retreat, but a longer class, in the summer term. This course is designed to give students a retreat experience and then the opportunity to learn about retreat design and leadership. We read current literature, analyze the retreat experience we had together, discuss different forms of worship appropriate on retreat, and explore all the questions that arise as the students begin to design their own retreats and prepare to lead them.

As my interest in retreats has taken a professional turn, I continue to attend to my own rhythm of retreats. I have discovered that leading a retreat is no substitute for being on retreat. Every spring I go for a full week to a small mountain house for a week of solitude. In summer, fall, and winter I either go to a retreat house for a day or two, attend a guided retreat at a local church, or spend a day alone in nature. It is important to me that I practice what I teach.

CONTEMPLATIVE RETREATS AND CONGREGATIONAL LIFE

As longing for silence and solitude grows in our wider culture, as new retreat houses are being built and many existing ones are reserved months in advance, the Protestant community needs to be informed and educated about the retreat movement. I have heard much confusion and misinformation about contemplative retreats:

Retreats are a Catholic thing.
Retreats are for Buddhists.
People who go on retreat are trying to escape the real
    world.
People who go on retreat think they are "holier than thou."
People who go on retreat have nothing else to do.
Our church does retreats. We go off every year and plan the
    program and moan about the budget.

Our church goes on retreat. We help out at the local church camp
and have cookouts and talent shows and make new friends.
Our church is involved in social action; we have no time for retreats.

There is some truth in all of these statements. Retreats have long been
a part of the Catholic and Buddhist traditions. People go on retreat for all sorts
of reasons, some of them not particularly useful to themselves or others.
Churches do sponsor events that focus on vision, planning, service, or
fellowship. These statements, however, and the truths that they hold do not
reflect the way I will be using the term retreat in this book. For me, a retreat
is about God. A retreat places God and the things of God in the foreground
of our attention. A retreat opens the time and the space so that we may hear
God's still, small voice. A retreat is about listening and waiting, receiving and
being. A retreat is not about getting anything done.

On retreat we may find clarity. On retreat we may make friends and build
community. Plans may grow from retreat time. We may even have fun. But
what occurs during or after a time away is not the purpose of retreat. We go
on retreat simply to be with God. I will use the descriptive word
"contemplative" to distinguish this retreat from other types of retreats. A
contemplative retreat gives us the opportunity to practice spending time in the
presence of the God who loves us.

Because the Catholic Church already has within its tradition many
contemplative resources, this book is designed primarily for Protestant
church leaders who desire to make contemplative retreats an integral part of
their congregational life but lack the resources our Catholic friends enjoy.
Although I trust the book will be of equal value for those who are designing
and leading ecumenical retreats and for those who wish to create a structure
for their private solitary retreats, I have chosen the former focus for a number
of reasons.

Members of congregations are exploring retreats outside their
worshiping communities. They are going to Catholic retreat houses on their
own. They are attending group retreats in nature. Many are going off on
retreats by themselves. These experiences may be valuable, but many
Protestants long to share retreats with members of their own congregations,
and they do not know how.

Contemplative retreats and other spiritual formation activities strengthen
a congregation. As members attend to their individual prayer lives, or join
together to discern the movement of the spirit in their individual and corporate

lives, a subtle, pervasive vitality begins to flow throughout church activities. One woman, a participant in contemplative activities of her church, said, "For me, the core mission of the church is to spread God's love and God's peace in a hurting world. If you can't feel it, can't know it, it's a lot harder to spread it. The more time you spend in the heart of God, the more love and peace you have to give."

Contemplative activities serve as an outreach to the unchurched of our communities. Many people are longing for information and experiences in spiritual formation and development and do not consider themselves religious. They have stayed away from our churches because they believe the church has nothing spiritual to offer them. Contemplative activities also attract members of other Christian denominations, thus building a spirit of ecumenism in a community.

HOW TO USE THIS BOOK

As you anticipate designing and leading contemplative retreats, as you read the following chapters and make use of the resources provided, do not simply read this book as one more good idea for a church program. Introducing and encouraging the contemplative life within a congregation need to be done by those who are engaged in their own spiritual formation. Before you attempt to bring the contemplative dimension into others' lives, find a retreat to attend. Become a participant in a prayer group. Immerse yourself in books that nurture your soul. Practice silence. Discover Sabbath. Attend to the Holy in all you do. The contemplative life is "caught not taught." Only in nurturing your own relationship with God can you become the catalyst for others.

Because this book will focus on the local church, chapter 1 tells the story of one congregation that has a contemplative retreat program. Through interviews with the pastor, with members of the congregation, and with people outside the congregation who attend some of the contemplative offerings, the story unfolds. How the program started, what changes occurred within the congregation, and the ways the church met the many needs of a diverse congregation are told. Those interviewed speak about how the contemplative life of the church helped to heal a congregational split. They wrestle with the integration of the contemplative, the intellectual, and the active dimensions of the church. This real life story will present a church that values many different ways of exploring the contemplative life before we turn our attention to the specific task of designing and leading contemplative retreats.

Chapter 2 explores the full meaning of the word "contemplative." Drawing on both ancient and contemporary sources, we will explore what it means to be a contemplative in the world today. At the heart of the contemplative life are the practices of silence, listening, and receptivity, which we will discuss in light of our noisy, wordy, active world.

A contemplative retreat differs from other retreats because of its shape as well as its purpose. Chapter 3 will explore a model that provides structure for retreat participants to find the space to wait for God. How retreatants experience waiting, how they discover what they are waiting for, and how they make the transition back to a more active life will be shared.

Chapter 4 will focus on contemplative retreat leadership and how it differs from preaching, teaching, facilitating, or chairing a meeting. The qualities of a retreat leader will be outlined, and ways to develop effective retreat leaders will be discussed. Particular issues for retreat leaders, such as developing a sense of timing, speaking less rather than more, and responding to retreatants' emotions, will be explored.

The structure of a retreat depends on a carefully planned schedule in which retreatants are freed to explore their relationship with God. Chapter 5 will discuss how to create a spacious schedule, how to balance solitary and communal experiences, and how to create worship experiences that are congruent with contemplation. Sample retreat schedules are included.

What do people do on a contemplative retreat where so much time is spent in silence? Chapter 6 will suggest themes for retreats and present a variety of activities that are appropriate for contemplative retreats, such as guided meditation, spiritual direction, physical activities, different forms of prayer, and the practice of lectio divina.

Chapter 7 explores the fruits of contemplative retreats for individuals and churches. People who have been on retreats will share their experiences, and pastors whose churches are involved with retreat ministry will reflect on their understanding of the effects of retreat ministries on their congregations.

The book concludes with two appendices. Appendix A presents an outline for a home retreat to meet the needs of those who cannot go away but wish to explore the contemplative life. Appendix B includes resources for your own spiritual growth, music and books for worship preparation, and ways to find suitable retreat houses.

My prayer for you as you read this book is to discover within yourself the longing for the contemplative life. Perhaps you will realize that the unnamed longing of your heart now has a name. Maybe you will find, as I did, that you are already a contemplative. Some of you may find the ideas in this book new and unfamiliar, and others may experience a sense of coming home. I urge all of you to read with open and discerning minds and hearts, taking from my thoughts and experiences and stories that which will feed your soul and perhaps give you some concrete ideas of ways to nurture the life of the Spirit within your own congregations.

ACKNOWLEDGMENTS

I wish to express gratitude to the following people:

- Beth Gaede at the Alban Institute, who first approached me about writing this book and proceeded to edit it with clear vision, good humor, and grace.
- The Louisville Institute for supporting the project by granting me financial assistance.
- Cathie Woehl, who, after typing three books for me, has become a friend as well as a secretary.
- The folks at First Congregational Church in Colorado Springs, who graciously shared their experiences, observations, memories, and stories with me: Lucy Bell, Sarah Bender, Flo W. Carris, Siri Everett, Jerusha Goebel, Ruth Heine, Ceil Malek, Betty Lynn and Lynn Mahaffy-Boudreau, Gary Rapp, Dave Seyfert, Becky Weiss, Cathy White, Jim White, and Gene D. Yelken.
- The students in my two Retreat Ministry classes who helped me articulate many of the ideas in this book through their probing questions, their own experiences of retreat, and their creative projects: Kathryn Andrews, Mary Bielass, Kurt Borgaard, Susan Carabajal, Sonja Craven, Siri Everett, David Ferguson, Jane Anne Ferguson, Doug Kraft, Leah McCullough, Joanne Parkhouse, Julia Parmenter, Carolyn Peters, Mark Peterson, Sharyl Peterson, Bruce Pratt, Jann Schwab, Robert Simpson, and Kay Young.
- The participants in the Sounds of Silence and Practice of Presence retreats who responded to my questionnaires and provided many of the stories and examples that enliven the theory of retreat design and leadership.

- The priests and staff of the Sacred Heart Jesuit Retreat House for their hospitality and the use of one of their hermitages to work in protected silence and solitude.
- Swanee Hunt for the use of the cabin at Columbine ranch and the caretakers Bud and Kathy Jankiewicz who made me comfortable and left me alone while I wrote.
- Kay Young for writing the annotated Music Resources; Trish Dunn, Jim Laurie, and Sharyl Peterson for editorial assistance; Kelby Cotton, Tom Esselman, Mary Hulst, Paul Laurie, Tren Meyers, Kathy Mordeaux, Margaret Johnson, Nora Smith, and Vie Thorgren for ideas and stories that are scattered across these pages.

This book, in this form, could not have been written without your hard work, your stories, and your support and encouragement. Thank you.

CHAPTER 1

A CHURCH WITH SOUL

Responding to God's love, we are First Congregational United Church of Christ, an inclusive, ecumenical and spiritual people, who through worship, learning, community and outreach seek to embrace the Mystery of God.

Mission Statement
First Congregational
United Church of Christ

This mission statement of First Congregational Church, a 650-member congregation near the center of downtown Colorado Springs, is the outcome of nearly a decade of self-reflection. At the heart of this reflection was an intentional emphasis on the spiritual life of the congregation. The spiritual focus began quietly and slowly with a simple question from a new church member. Over the years the spiritual interests of a few have expanded to touch every aspect of congregational life and are now being felt beyond the church walls in the wider community.

The question came from Siri Everett soon after she and her family joined the church. She approached the pastor, Jim White, and asked, "Do we have a centering prayer group here?" "No," he replied. "Let's start one." Siri had come to her faith through a mystical conversion and had been searching for a way to respond to God's invitation to intimacy. She had encountered centering prayer at a neighboring monastery and had recognized that particular prayer form as the response she had been seeking. But she wanted to practice her prayer within her Protestant community. Hence, her question to Jim.

Unknown to Siri, Jim had been practicing centering prayer for years but had done nothing to bring his contemplative interest into his intellectual and socially active congregation. Siri's invitation was all he needed. Jim set aside an evening for a meeting to discuss the spiritual life of the congregation. He sent an open invitation to the congregation to attend the discussion. Only a few people showed up that evening, but there were enough to form a committee they named the Spiritual Life Committee.

Eventually, this committee became an official part of the Worship Council. In this church the Worship Council oversees and coordinates the work of the Music Committee, the Communion Committee, the Sanctuary Arts Committee and the Sunday Services Committee. Adding this committee to the Worship Council placed the spiritual well-being of the congregation within the structure of the church. As a formal part of the church, the spiritual life of individual members and of the total congregation is not entirely dependent on particular people and their interest in contemplation. Lay leaders or clergy may come and go, but the importance of spirituality will remain in the church. The organizational change has been instrumental in the slow but steady progress this congregation has made in providing a wide range of spiritual activities.

"We were a small band to begin with," Siri remembers, "with a big heart." They had little money to spend but plenty of ideas. They began with the original plan to form a centering prayer group, which continues, along with a second group, to this day. One participant said, "It's the most natural way to worship that I have ever found. At times it's like being aware of God's overwhelming presence. Those of us who attend consistently look forward to it, and we don't miss unless something very important interferes." Jim is one of the regular prayers. His faithfulness to the group and to prayer is important to the participants. Although the groups are small in numbers, there is a sense that having the groups meeting regularly for prayer in the church building supports the rest of the congregation as well as those who attend.

CONTEMPLATIVE RETREATS

The interest in contemplative prayer led the Spiritual Life Committee to sponsor a contemplative retreat. "This church had had retreats before, but not contemplative retreats. Our women's retreats were very social. They were like a big pajama party. They were fun, but this was something new," one church member recalled. The first retreat was held at the Benedictine Monastery in Snowmass, Colorado, where the small group of retreatants gathered to pray together, walk in the glory of nature, eat meals in silence, and attend services with the monks. They shared their spiritual journeys with one another and returned from the retreat feeling closer to each other and to God.

Regular contemplative retreats have been held since that time. The committee has discovered a variety of sites for retreat, and they have called on different people both from within and outside their congregation for leadership. Sometimes the retreats have a theme, such as "Belonging" or "Compassion." Other times the retreat centers around the contemplative study of one Scripture passage, such as a psalm or a story from the Gospels. The one constant in the contemplative retreats is the long periods of silence.

The experience of silence provides something important to the retreatants. "I love the silence," exclaimed a church member who shares her musical gifts with the congregation. "I go off the scale as an extrovert, so it's hard. But something innately hungers for it. I am not afraid of the silence. I am afraid of the noise! I have slowly come to peace with my internal chatter so I no longer feel compelled to get rid of it. I now know how to be with it until it quiets and fades away to nothing."

"The church's contemplative movement provides me with little islands of silence that I neglect to provide for myself," another church member confided. "When I am on retreat and when I come back, I am always aware of being loved by God in a deeper way. I get in touch with my lovableness in that silence."

"The retreats have been enormously important to me. They tend to fuel me for a long time," a teacher of English mused. "It's interesting that I am a writer, but have very little language for my contemplative retreat experiences. What happens is I let go of all language and get to some other place where language isn't. I think language sets the stage for my contemplative experiences, but the contemplative experiences themselves have no words attached."

People who have been on contemplative retreats together develop a connection even when few words are spoken. But the words that are shared seem to come from a deeper place. They feel more authentic and closer to the soul. A church lay leader, new to retreats, said with amazement, "When you go on retreat with someone, you cannot help but become friends, for you both believe in the contemplative dimension of the Christian life. Then the Holy Spirit, who draws us to God, draws us lovingly to one another."

ADDITIONAL CONTEMPLATIVE EXPERIENCES

Because of the closeness that was growing among those who had shared retreat time together, the Spiritual Life Committee realized that there was a danger of being perceived as "special" or as a "closed" group. They knew many people could not get away for a weekend and that others were not interested in the weekend retreat model, so they sought to expand their vision and understanding of contemplative retreats. They actively sought out new members for the committee. They explored ways of being a committee that modeled the spiritual life they were seeking to promote. Meetings began with devotions and intentional invocation of the presence of God. Like all committees, tasks had to be done, jobs needed to be assigned, money had to be raised and allocated. But as one woman reported after serving in the kitchen during a daylong retreat, "There is a certain amount of housekeeping to be done, even in the spiritual life, but if you do the tasks by practicing the presence of God, it all comes out well in the end. I did not attend much of the actual retreat, but I came away as nurtured as if I had."

Together the committee tries to discern the movement of the Spirit in the congregation in order to understand the spiritual needs that exist. They try to respond to these felt needs, rather than simply coming up with their own spiritual agenda. A committee member reflected thoughtfully, "We have such a broad spectrum of religious and spiritual disciplines and interests in our church. They all need to be recognized and honored, and opportunities should be offered to people to participate in a variety of ways." Out of this discernment and the committee's commitment to diversity, a number of spiritual activities have emerged in addition to the centering prayer groups and the weekend retreats.

In 1997 the Spiritual Life Committee, with the blessing of the Worship Council, decided to make a labyrinth of canvas for their social hall. Half of the money for its construction came from sources outside the church, including a Buddhist prayer group, an Episcopal church, and a Benedictine community.

The diagram on the following page is a representation of the labyrinth found in the nave of Chartres Cathedral in France. The labyrinth is 41 feet in diameter and is a single path with twists and turns, but, unlike a maze, it is not designed to trap or trick. Walking the labyrinth symbolizes walking with God and walking toward God. It is a metaphoric pilgrimage to the New Jerusalem.

First Congregational Church saw this contemplative tool as a way to meet the spiritual needs of those who could not retreat over a weekend and those who could not attend either the early morning or the late afternoon centering prayer group. The committee members also believed that the labyrinth would be a gift their church could give to the wider community.

Making a labyrinth is a huge project. A large space is needed to lay out the canvas. Many people are needed to place the design on the canvas in the exact dimensions. And after the pattern is drawn, it must be painted. All of this work is done on hands and knees. In addition, plans must be made for storing and transporting the completed labyrinth.

A church member who was a schoolteacher received permission to use the school gymnasium for a weekend. Those who had signed up to help gathered at the school. "The making of the labyrinth was a contemplative experience," she remembers. "We prayed together as we began, and then throughout the day we would have periods of reflection, more times of prayer, and then we would return to working and playing, drawing and painting."

The labyrinth is available to the community one late afternoon a week. During Holy Week it is open for walking every day. The labyrinth is also available on New Year's Eve. Someone from the church is always there to welcome people and explain the purpose of the labyrinth to newcomers. Silence is maintained, and candles are available if people wish to walk holding the light. "I went to the labyrinth in sorrow about having to make a life decision," a woman in midlife shared. "I picked up a candle and walked slowly and quietly to the center where I sat to pray. It became clear to me that just carrying my light was enough. I left the labyrinth knowing that all would be well; I simply needed to carry my light."

A mother of teenagers described dancing the labyrinth with her daughter: "I wanted to introduce her to the spiritual life, and the labyrinth seemed the perfect way. We were there alone and we got fairly wild, stomping and bopping and having great fun." In the middle of their experience, a woman came in to walk the labyrinth for the first time. When watching the pair, she realized there was no right way to walk the labyrinth. She found her own style, her own path, and broke out of her need to "do it right." She told them later that their exuberance that night had helped her "color outside the lines."

Some people like to walk the labyrinth alone; others find it exciting to be on the journey with fellow travelers. "When I walk with others, I feel like I am both observing and being a part of a microcosm of life," a student of the contemplative life wrote. "Young and old, we are all on a journey. We meet each other, we turn away. We move at different speeds, each of us with our own distinctive pacing and body postures. I have the feeling that we are notes in a symphony, slow whole notes, fast eighth notes, high and low notes, but all a part of the same great piece."

The labyrinth has gotten so much use that the church is considering placing the pattern permanently on the floor of the social hall. "This floor has needed to be replaced for years," I was told by a church member. "It is a perfect time to construct a permanent labyrinth. We will be just like Chartres Cathedral!"

Another spiritual offering of First Congregational Church are Taizé worship services. At present they are being held quarterly, as well as at the beginning of Advent, on Ash Wednesday, and on Pentecost. The Taizé services are designed on the model of the Taizé community in France, which was founded in 1940 to help Jews fleeing Nazis and which later became a place of reconciliation after the devastation of World War II.

The Taizé service is built around music that has a simple refrain and is sung over and over again. The repetition quiets the mind and leads the worshippers into silent, meditative prayer. Most Taizé services also include the reading of Scripture, spoken prayer, and periods of silence. First Congregational Church has added a ritual of healing to its services. "People come from all over the city to these services of music and prayer and healing," one of the Taizé worship leaders said. "There is a hunger out there for contemplative experiences. We feel great gratitude that we can do something to meet that need."

From the beginning, the Taizé services have always included young people. Youth have been included as vocalists, instrumentalists, readers, and members of the healing prayer teams. Because of this experience, contemplative practices are being introduced into Sunday school classes and into the junior-high and high-school youth groups. "As we adults feel more assured and experienced in our spiritual practices," the mother of three young people wrote, "it becomes easier and more compelling to teach them to the beloved children in our congregation."[1]

Another avenue into the spiritual life is the church's Adult Forum, which is a Sunday school class that is held between the traditional Sunday services. The forum has been facilitated for 18 years by Dave Seyfert, a member of the congregation, and has covered a wide range of religious, political, theological, and spiritual issues. The forum often runs series of four to six weeks, using books, speakers, or current events. The format is to have 20 minutes of presentation, then give-and-take among the participants for the rest of the hour. "Dave has a very nurturing way of making a place for people to investigate matters of religion and spirituality," a regular participant said. "There is a real feeling of investigation and discovery in the forum sessions."

Many members of this church wish to explore issues of spirituality cognitively, through their minds. They do not go on retreats or walk the labyrinth or attend Taizé services. This does not mean they are not interested in the contemplative life. They want to think about it, read about it, talk about it. The forum gives them an opportunity to do that. "Spirituality is the topic that tends to draw the most interest these days," Dave told me. "We have looked at spirituality from various perspectives and tried to peel away the layers to see if we can understand this thing called spirituality. We offer opportunities for people to express doubts, disagree with each other, or take issue with 'official doctrine.' We welcome that kind of discussion."

Film is another avenue into the spiritual life being explored at First Congregational Church. Jim picks the films with the help of a committee. When people watch the films, they are invited to not only enjoy the story and look for theological implications, they are encouraged to allow the images to guide them inward. Discussing the film helps people share their own spiritual questions and insights and stories.

Pastoral Leadership

In all these activities, Jim has been encouraging and supportive, attending as many of the events as his busy schedule allows. "The Spiritual Life Committee has been a very active group," Jim reported. "They are not dependent on me." But the committee and the congregation believe that without Jim's contemplative understanding and experience, the church could not have developed the spiritual depth that it has. "Ten days before Easter, Jerusha Goebel presented the Spiritual Life Committee with the idea of holding an all-night vigil on Holy Thursday," a member of the committee remembered. "Although some thought it was too last minute, we told her to run it by Jim. When she laid out her plan, he simply said, 'Jerusha, I love this!' The committee worked hard to make it happen, and we had a truly Holy Thursday."

Sunday worship and Jim's leadership are being affected by the contemplative activities. Film themes show up in sermons. Taizé chants sometimes replace a hymn. Periods of silence have lengthened. But the focus of the Sunday service remains the sermon. "Jim's sermons are very intellectual. They always have been and always will be. They are important to the life of the church. People come particularly to hear him preach," a retired pastor and a member of the church said. "Jim is an intellectual. He is also a contemplative. Jim serves as a good model who proves that you don't have to give up your intelligence to be a person of prayer."

Jim is also a social activist, and First Congregational Church has always been a large-issues church. Many people first attend and then join the church because of its witness to justice and peace. The recent emphasis on spirituality has created no conflict with service projects of the church. In fact, many people believe that social action is being encouraged by the prayers of the community. "The contemplative activities of the church help us to listen to where God is calling us into action," the father of two preschoolers shared. "We are not a large church; we cannot meet every need. We need to allow our hearts, touched by God, to lead us into action."

"It is only logical to have contemplation at the heart of any kind of outreach. Contemplation deepens compassion," a junior high school teacher shared thoughtfully. "When we serve from compassion, we may not have a bigger program, but it will be richer and more intentional and will be coming much more from the place of Christ within." Another member added, "I have to have quiet time in order to do good work. I think that's true for the church as a whole. There has to be some amount of quiet introspection nourishing us—a drinking from the fountain, if you will. Only then will we be able to stand up and do what needs to be done."

First Congregational Church is a community open to protecting the legal rights of gay and lesbian persons. The General Synod of the United Church of Christ has long urged congregations along this line. Such openness became a prophetic stance in the conservative environment of Colorado Springs when Colorado Amendment 2 (which essentially denied civil rights to lesbians and gays) came before the people of Colorado in 1992. Even so, there was considerable dissension within the church regarding full acceptance of gay and lesbian persons. The different opinions crystallized in the debate over whether to permit holy union ceremonies for lesbian and gay couples, and later, whether to become an Open and Affirming Church, which indicates that the church welcomes full participation of gay, lesbian, and bisexual people in all parts of congregational life. The church divided over these issues. People felt unheard, some people left, some unhappily remained, and others were enlivened by the position the church took in this matter. The church leaders invited a consultant to help with conflict resolution and peacemaking, and because of the particular methods she chose to use, the situation got worse rather than better.

A group of people who had been involved in the contemplative activities of the church came together to pray. Out of their prayer time, they decided to use blessed oil to anoint the church. "We started at the altar," Jerusha told me. "We anointed the pews, we anointed the windows, we anointed Jim and the staff. We reconsecrated the whole church to God. At the end we joined hands around the altar and prayed and cried. Our tears fell on the glass that covers the altar, and as we ended, we started to wipe away the tears. Someone said, 'No, leave the tears on the altar where they belong.'"

Many people mark the beginning of the healing of the church with the anointing ritual. It placed God, rather than hurts and opinions and anger and fear, back at the center of the church. It reminded those who were active in different forms of prayer to return in earnest to their prayer lives. It encouraged people to pray for the congregation, which led one active member to comment, "It is so powerful knowing that folks are holding this church in prayer. I'm not sure we knew what that meant before." An older, retired member added, "I would say we are coming out of the valley and being resurrected as a church. There is a lot of enthusiasm and a certain amount of fun. Jim's leadership has been prayerful, steady, fearless, and stubborn."

HEALING AND GROWING

Many years have passed since that first question was asked: "Do we have a centering prayer group here?" The inquiry and the response began the church's journey into the experience of contemplative retreats, to the formation of the Spiritual Life Committee, and to the development of other contemplative programs. These contemplative experiences provided a touchstone to the people and the minister of a church in crisis. They knew how to return to prayer. They knew how to discover compassion. They knew that words and more words would not be the answer. They knew they could not resolve their differences without God's help. The church is not healed, but it is healing. New people are attending, some because of the emphasis on spirituality, others because of the church's social witness, others because it is in the neighborhood and seems like a good place to be. Membership has increased from 440 in 1993 to 650 in 1999.

First Congregational Church of Colorado Springs is an ordinary church in many ways. It has a beautiful old building that needs care. It never has quite enough money to do all that members would like. Volunteers are often in short supply. But First Congregational is a church that is visible. Its mission is clear. People across denominational and religious lines are welcomed and attend its services and take part in its activities. As one visitor said after attending a Sunday morning service, "This church has soul."

CHAPTER 2

BECOMING CONTEMPLATIVE

To be silent and to listen befits the disciple.

Rule of Benedict

"I am not a contemplative." I spoke those words some years ago before a large group of Protestant clergy during a panel discussion following a presentation by Father Thomas Keating on the method and practice of centering prayer. A friend and colleague asked me later why I had said that. She told me that she knew me to be deeply contemplative and wondered why I had denied it.

My friend's gentle confrontation invited me to self-examination. I realized I could not call myself a contemplative because of an image I held of what a contemplative looked like. According to my mental picture, a contemplative was able to sit still for a long time, could clear the mind of all thoughts and images, practiced at a regular time faithfully every day, and had some sort of a privileged relationship with God. I was sorely lacking in all four of these criteria. Since my friend believed I was a contemplative, maybe I needed a new image. My search for this new image opened me to a deeper understanding of the contemplative life.

DEFINING CONTEMPLATION

St. Augustine said that contemplation is "the striving to understand those things that really and supremely are."[1] Because I believe experience is as valuable as understanding, I have expanded Augustine's concept and use the following working definition of contemplation: "Contemplation is the striving to understand and experience those things that really and supremely are." "Those things that really and supremely are" could be further defined as "those things that are God and those things that are of God." If we simplify the sentence, we now have: "Contemplation is the striving to understand and experience God."

To define contemplation in this way brings to mind an entirely different image of a contemplative than the one I initially held. Based on this image, I am comfortable calling myself a contemplative, because I see that my attitude is much more important than a particular practice or set of behaviors. This definition makes room for and affirms the many ways one strives to understand and experience God. It allows dancing and swimming and walking as well as sitting still. It allows thinking and questioning and imagining as well as an empty mind. It affirms that experiencing and understanding God and the things of God can occur anywhere and at any time, not only in prescribed periods of prayer. It implies that the contemplative has no "inside track" to God, but is simply one who yearns and seeks and strives to know God ever more deeply.

Our new definition places contemplation directly in the middle of our lives. This definition brings the concept of contemplation out of the realms of the extraordinary and into our ordinary existence. "Contemplation . . . is often misunderstood as occurring only during intense periods of prayer. . . . Yet contemplation is far more than that, and far more available to us. Contemplation is the weaving together of our daily lives and God's creative spirit."[2]

The Christian church has not always placed contemplation in the middle of daily activity. "St. Gregory of Nyssa (330-c.395) taught that the contemplative life is heavenly and cannot be lived in the world."[3] He understood the contemplative life to be reserved for monastics, to be practiced only behind monastery walls. Theologians of the eighteenth and nineteenth centuries removed contemplation even further from daily living by identifying it "with extraordinary phenomena, and regarding it as both miraculous and dangerous, to be admired from a safe distance."[4]

Some twentieth-century Christians have not viewed the contemplative life as dangerous, but rather as unnecessary. In their thinking, to know God is to realize God's kingdom on earth by working for peace and justice. They have separated contemplation from action and prayer from work.

Many Protestant and Catholic thinkers have tried to heal this artificial division between faith and action. "Contemplation blends vision and action so that each is informed and influenced by the other. Either without the other is incomplete, whether for contemplation or for life itself."[5] I, too, believe that most people of faith today experience contemplation in the midst of everyday life. We may retreat to remind ourselves of the graces of contemplation, but we always return to love and serve each other and the world.

THE CONTEMPLATIVE JESUS

To overcome twenty centuries of confused and often contradictory teachings about contemplation, we can return to the person of Jesus to provide us with an image of the true contemplative. Richard Foster writes:

> Jesus, who retreated often into the rugged wilderness, who lived and worked praying, who heard and did only what the Father said and did, shows forth the Contemplative Tradition in its fullness and utter beauty.[6]

Jesus' life was one of striving to understand and experience God. From his childhood experience in the temple (Luke 2:41-52), to his baptism in the river Jordan by John the Baptist (Luke 3:21-22), to his sojourn into the desert before the beginning of his ministry (Luke 4:1-13), Jesus was searching for and opening himself to God. During his ministry Jesus was in deep communion with God. "I can do nothing on my own," he said. "As I hear, I judge; and my judgment is just, because I seek to do not my own will but the will of him who sent me" (John 5:30). In his prayers on the Mount of Olives, Jesus struggled with his knowledge that he must die on the cross (Luke 22:39-46). Finally, in the moment before his death, he cried out to his God, "Father, into your hands I commend my spirit" (Luke 23:46).

Jesus' intimacy with his Abba was experienced in the midst of his studying, his teaching, his feasting, his healing. Jesus was a contemplative in his living and in his dying. But he also took time apart. "In the morning, while it was still very dark, he got up and went out to a deserted place, and there he prayed" (Mark 1:35). In Luke's gospel we read that "he would withdraw to deserted places and pray" (Luke 5:16). The word "places" indicates that withdrawal into prayer was a regular practice for Jesus. Jesus also encouraged his disciples to withdraw from the constancy of ministry to renew themselves. "The apostles gathered around Jesus, and told him all that they had done and taught. He said to them, 'Come away to a deserted place all by yourselves and rest a while.' For many were coming and going, and they had no leisure even to eat" (Mark 6:30-31).

Jesus withdrew to pray and he taught his disciples to "come away." Jesus knew God to be with him and his followers as they traveled throughout the land spreading the good news. He also knew that in the midst of such activity, he would not be able to give God the constant and devoted attention that nourished him to his very soul. So he went away. He withdrew. He sought out deserted places. He found ways to be silent and still in the presence of his God. Then he returned to his demanding ministry filled with an experience of God's faithful and abiding love.

Jesus' words and his life encourage us to find for ourselves a rhythm of retreat. In the midst of our busy lives we need moments or hours or days away to renew ourselves in the presence of God. With all the noise that surrounds us, we often long for quiet and to obey the psalmist's command to "be still before the Lord and wait. . . ." (Ps. 37:7). We do not long to withdraw in order to escape our lives. We yearn for the time and the space apart to focus our full loving attention on God so that we can return to our lives filled with the peace and the joy that comes only from God. Time away develops within us "a growing light, a growing awareness, a growing confidence both in God and ourselves."[7] To develop a contemplative life, we need contemplative retreats.

EXPERIENCING SILENCE

A contemplative retreat can be as short as a breath or as long as a month. In some Buddhist traditions people may go on retreat for years. Contemplative retreats may have the form of a prayer group, a walk on the labyrinth, an hour on a park bench, a day of quiet at home, a weekend in a retreat house. Whatever the form or content or length of the retreat, the one constant in a contemplative retreat is silence.

Silence is hard to find in our culture. Our homes may be filled with the whining of kitchen appliances, the clanking of exercise equipment, and the beeping of computers. People carry their own boom boxes. Cars play stereos at top volume. Neighborhoods are filled with power lawn mowers, leaf blowers, and snowblowers. City streets sport garbage trucks, jackhammers, and backfiring buses. Whistles blow, sirens shriek, horns honk, and helicopters fly overhead. Stores play music continually, people talk through movies and concerts, and cell phones ring in church

We long for silence and yet we are afraid of silence. For when the outer world is quiet, we begin to hear our inner noise. Our heads are filled with chatter, our hearts with emotions. We replay history and rehearse the future. We wander away from the present moment by making lists, or planning supper, or anticipating an argument, or remembering who said what to whom at yesterday's meeting. In the silence we begin to realize that we are everywhere but here.

Another reason some people are afraid of silence is because they have been wounded by silence. Silence can be used in relationships as a weapon. "When my wife is angry with me, she gives me 'the silent treatment.' I don't know what I have done, and I feel uneasy and on edge," one man reported. A young woman shared that her father used to clam up, not speak during dinner, not wish her goodnight. Her father's silence frightened her because it was usually followed by an explosion of anger. Another woman remembered the silence of a friend that was hurtful: "My friend would get quiet and then just walk away and leave me if I said something to displease her."

Silence can also wound us when we have been silenced by another. Most of us have been told at some time: "Keep quiet!" "Shhhhh." "Lower your voice." "Shut up!" For some, the wounding is deeper. "My stepfather would shout at me to shut up, and if I kept on talking, he would slap me across the face," a teacher shared, her pain visible on her face. "No wonder I am afraid of silence and words." Another retreatant confessed, "My uncle told me not to tell anyone after he fondled me. He threatened me. For me, silence is filled with dirty secrets."

For people who have been wounded by silence, solitary silence may be comfortable, but silence in community feels too close to painful memories. Listen to these brief stories: "Eating in silence with others is still very uncomfortable for me, even after three days. It is too much like the meals in my family of origin, where everyone was afraid to speak." "When I sit down next to someone and they don't speak to me, I feel rejected, even though I know that no one is talking to anyone." "When we are together in the kitchen, I feel an almost compulsive urge to fill the silence with chatter. I think I am looking for the approval I never got from my mother."

Another way silence frightens us is that silence makes us vulnerable.

Words can be used to build relationships if we share from the depths of who we are. But frequently words are used to defend ourselves, to protect ourselves from intimacy. "I use words to attack," an attorney told me. "When I am silent, I feel I have no protection, no weapon. I am vulnerable and I feel weak." When we talk constantly and fill the silence with words, we do not need to listen or relate. When we are silent with another, we may hear that person's pain and sorrow; we may witness that person's wonder and joy. Such heartfelt listening moves us toward intimacy, and intimacy makes us vulnerable.

Those of us who use words in our teaching, preaching, and writing can also fear silence because we believe ourselves to be defined by language. We become identified with the spoken or written word. We are expected to be able to offer a meaningful closing prayer at the end of a gathering. We are asked for articulate summaries of long discussions. Our words of wisdom are eagerly awaited. People wonder if they can quote us. We begin to think we are our words. "I was afraid of silence because I believed I was loved for my words," a published writer reported. "I was afraid that without words I would not be loved. What a joy to experience deep regard from others without saying a word."

Our past experiences with silence will influence the way we respond to silence on retreat. Our personality type may also affect our response to silence. "Sometimes it is said that introverts long for silence and solitude, and extroverts flee silence and solitude,"[8] wrote Reuben Job in his book *Spiritual Life in the Congregation*. The invitation to silence may elicit these responses initially, but both personality types can learn to receive the gift of silence. A highly extroverted retreatant wrote that she had feared that she would not be able to maintain silence and might negatively affect the participation of others; however, she "found the silence to be welcoming, comforting, and rich with inner growth." An introverted retreatant also made a delightful discovery in the silent community: "I am an introvert by definition; that is, I restore my energy alone. But I love relationships as well. This experience afforded me the best of all worlds."

FRUITS OF SILENCE

When silence is practiced in a safe community, healing can occur. People understand that the silence is not commanded, nor is it a punishment. It holds no secrets. People begin to look at one another without words between them and learn what it is to truly see and be seen. "The silence of this retreat offered me a safe place to experience a deep prevailing sadness for which I had no words," a student reflected. "The raw recollection of being silenced over the years began to feel personally tragic. Memories prevailed of people protecting themselves with cynicism, body language, 'the silent treatment,' ridicule, humor and 'put-downs.' The contemplative atmosphere freed me and inspired me. We became an intimate group sharing our mutual intent to listen to God."

With healing comes the possibility of embracing silence and allowing silence to embrace us so that we can turn our attention to God. Silence is not the purpose of a contemplative retreat, but rather the vehicle for paying attention to God. Often we discover God through our senses, which come alive in silence. We seem to see and hear more clearly the created world around us. We also see and hear each other on deeper levels.

As our senses open and we take time to see and hear and touch and taste and smell, we may experience gratitude. "We eat our meals in silence to make it easier to give our full attention to the food and to the other members of the community who are present," wrote Thich Naht Hanh about life in Buddhist monasteries. "Every time we eat a meal, gratitude is our practice."[9] Gratitude expands from mealtime to include all we experience on retreat, such as the sound of rain, the warmth of a fire, the smile of another, the weight of a warm quilt on a cold night, the smell of bread baking, the sparkle of dew drops, the turn of a phrase in a book we are reading.

When we do not need to share our experience, point it out to another, explain it, or expound upon it, we can simply be with whatever is happening and know it to be a gift from God. When we notice and pay attention to unpleasant things, such as a memory that hurts, the sight of litter, the sounds of an argument, the smell of pollution, or the continual barking of a dog, we can also practice gratitude for any new awareness we receive. "I was so annoyed by that ticking clock when I first arrived," a retreatant shared. "I wanted to rip it off the wall. But I became aware of how often small and unimportant things frustrate me and stir up my anger, so I practiced embracing the clock as part of my retreat experience. I am now rather fond of it."

On a contemplative retreat, leaders do not usually expect absolute, continual silence. Rather the silence is interspersed with times to talk and share. The retreat leader may present material for reflection or read aloud something for inspiration. During prescribed times for talking, participants may share their experiences with each other or with the retreat leader in spiritual direction. Sometimes spontaneous sharing occurs. "One moonlit night four of us 'escaped' to the gazebo and chatted and laughed and giggled, which was a wonderful mid-retreat release," a retreatant remembered with delight.

Words that grow in the silence seem to be more intentional and come from a deeper place within. In the silence we can find a truer voice and discover what we want to say. We find ways to speak that communicate and connect rather than fill space, defend, or confuse. This balance of silence and speech builds community. People experience deep connection with other retreatants, even though they know very little about the lives of one another. A bond is created within the group that grows from silence, intentional speech, and the shared experience of attending to God.

Although a professional basketball court may be far from the common understanding of a retreat setting, Phil Jackson, former head coach of the Chicago Bulls, discovered the power of silence in building teamwork. Jackson taught his team meditation as part of the team's daily practice.

> The experience of sitting silently together in a group tends to bring about a subtle shift in consciousness that strengthens the team bond. Sometimes we extend mindfulness to the court and conduct whole practices in silence. The deep level of concentration and nonverbal communication that arises when we do this never fails to astound me.[10]

LISTENING AND WAITING

"It's easy to pay attention to God," one retreatant told me on the second day of a retreat, "but how do I listen? I'm not sure what I am listening for." Another retreatant said, "When I listen for God, all I hear is myself!" In our relational lives, when we listen, we expect to hear something. When I listen to my stepson, I want to hear what he is saying. When I sit quietly in nature, I want to hear sounds. If I listen patiently, I may hear the rustle of a small animal or the cry of a coyote or the distant whistle of a train. I want to hear something.

When we listen to God, we simply listen. If prayer is attention without aim, as Simon Weil wrote, then prayer could as well be defined as "listening without expectation." Simply attending, simply listening. In fact, I am not sure that attending to God and listening for God are different. Both call us to the present moment. Both are ends in themselves. Both ask us to "show up" or to "put ourselves in the way of God." "Martin Heidegger said that true listening is worship. When you listen with your soul, you come into rhythm and unity with the music of the universe."[11]

A pastor friend said that when people pray with a constant flow of words, "God cannot get a word in edgewise." This is a delightful image, but it sets up the expectation that if we stop talking, God will speak, and God's words will be clear and intelligible. Father Thomas Keating is fond of saying that "silence was God's first language." I have always interpreted that phrase as a reminder to be silent in prayer, but I wonder if it also means that what we can expect from God is also silence. In an intimate relationship there are times when no words are necessary. Walking together in silence is joy. Reading different books in the same room creates closeness. As one woman put it, "Listening to God is like lying with my head on my lover's chest and listening to his heartbeat."

Contemplative retreats are about attending and listening and waiting for God. Contemplative retreats are about discovering stillness. We do these things while carrying on the activities of retreat. We listen and attend and wait as we chant and pray and sing and eat together. We listen and attend and wait while we walk alone, while we read, or do handwork, or watch the fire, or make our beds, or draw pictures, or write poetry, or simply do nothing. Contemplative retreats are not about accomplishing anything, getting somewhere, going home with the answers.

Early in my retreat experience I went away for six days of solitude. I was a little fearful, as I always am when I begin a retreat, for I never know what is going to happen. The days passed with an easy schedule of sleep and exercise, reading and prayer. I spent some time journaling and drawing and dancing. I walked in the beautiful environment, saw a deer one day, a small rabbit the next. After three days I began to get concerned. Nothing was happening. On other retreats I had had important insights, or tapped into my creativity, or worked through a problem in my life. A few retreats had been difficult. During one I had a series of disturbing dreams. At another I was agitated much of the time, unable to rest or relax or even find brief moments of peace. But on this retreat nothing was happening—nothing good and nothing bad.

Only in reflection after I had returned home did I realize the wonderful paradox that nothing happening was what happened! I simply went away and returned. I took time out to be with God, and I was with God. I was silent. God was silent. God was with me on retreat. God is with me in my everyday life. That retreat allowed me to practice the presence of God and taught me about the ordinariness of the contemplative life. As Thich Naht Hanh wrote, "The miracle is not to walk on water. The miracle is to walk on the green earth."[12]

Chapter 3

Shaping a Contemplative Retreat

*The soul instead of striving to engage in discourse strives to
remain attentive and aware of what the Lord is working in it.*

Teresa of Avila

Workshops, conferences, and action retreats are often designed to
produce a mountaintop experience. Somewhere near the end of the
program a culminating event occurs. A famous speaker may be flown in from
far away to provide participants some final wisdom. An elaborate worship
service with healing rituals and communion may be held. Someone might lead
a guided meditation for which participants were prepared through earlier
teachings and practices.

On the youth retreats I attended as a high school student, we always had
a campfire the final night. We sang and shared and witnessed to the faith
experiences we had discovered at camp. We hugged everyone and stayed
up all night filled with the wonder of the week and ourselves and each other
and God. We vowed to stay in touch and never let the experience fade. Then
in the morning, tired and sad, we got on our buses to go home.

There is nothing wrong with famous speakers, healing services,
meaningful group meditations, or campfires filled with joy and song. They are
simply illustrations of events that are shaped like this:

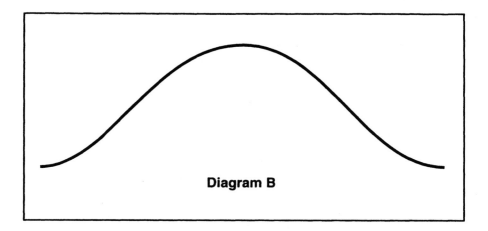

Diagram B

On a smaller scale, planning and problem solving and visioning events are also shaped in this way. Often a church leadership team or the faculty of a school or the managers of departments of a business will go away for a day of activities. When the event is held away from the church or school or office, it may be called a retreat. Usually these days away begin with food and informal fellowship. Sometimes community-building activities are included. The leader begins with a review of the issue, the problem, or the dream that is to be discussed and worked on that day. Maybe the history of what has gone before is presented.

The group then engages in a number of activities to gather opinions, express feelings, elicit new ideas, or generate enthusiasm for the project. Sometimes these activities are done in small groups, breakout sessions, or with the total group. In religious settings, time for individual prayer and reflection are sometimes included.

No matter the length of time, the number of people, or the activities chosen, these events are designed to accomplish something. Maybe a new budget is called for. Maybe a new configuration of the school day has to be decided upon. Maybe the church search committee is trying to discern the three top candidates for the senior pastor position. When the group accomplishes its task, the goal has been reached; the mountain has been conquered. The effort and the struggles are deemed worth it, the difficulties fade, and people rejoice together; however, if the group adjourns at the point of celebration, the shape of the event looks like this:

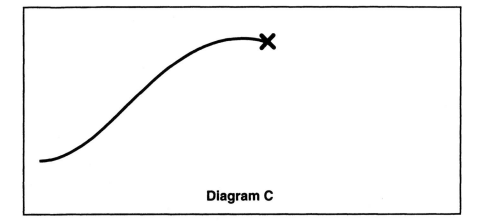

Diagram C

The wise leader takes as much care leading the group down the mountain as up the mountain. On the other side of celebration is some more hard work. People who do not totally endorse the final decision need to be attended to. How can they agree to cooperate even though the meeting did not go as they had hoped? What are the next steps to bringing the plan or the vision or the decision to those who will be affected by the results of the day? What resistance is anticipated? Going down the mountain is not as much fun as staying on the top.

I wonder how my youth camp experiences might have been different if the leaders had taken time to walk with us down the mountain. I'm sure I would not have wanted them to, for I loved the high spirits of the closing celebration. But what if the next morning before we got on the buses they helped us prepare for going home, helped us prepare to let go?

One youth counselor told me that he always led his group in a guided imagery about returning home. He asked them to imagine saying good-bye to people and places at the camp and to imagine the bus or car ride home. He asked them to remember who would greet them at home and how they felt about who and what was waiting for them. He asked them to imagine ways they could share their camp experience with those at home. An energetic discussion followed the activity and for most of the campers the transition had begun. "These kids are different after a week like this," he told me. "They have had powerful experiences. Going home can be a shock. I think if we prepare them, even a little, they may be able to stay connected to what they discovered here." This leader understood and facilitated the event model from beginning to end.

THE INVERTED SHAPE

A contemplative retreat includes many of the same elements as the previous event model. A contemplative retreat begins with food and fellowship and ends with careful transitional activities before retreatants leave for home. The difference is that the retreat shape is inverted. The image of the mountain is replaced by an image of depth.

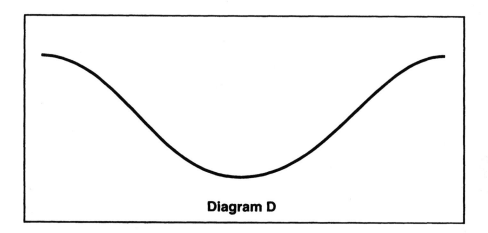

Diagram D

In the mountain model, activities are designed to help people ascend. In the contemplative retreat model, activities are designed to help people descend. Going up the mountain requires effort and willpower. Sinking into the depths requires surrender and letting go. To get up a mountain, adventurers need ways to keep their energy up. They need techniques for getting around boulders and over logs and finding the right trail. They need to work together, pulling together as a group. They need to keep their eyes on the top. Ultimately, their journey is about arriving.

To sink into the deep, adventurers need to be willing to step off solid ground. They need methods to help them let go of the known and familiar. They need to be willing to separate from the group and trust their own rhythms. They need to understand that they cannot perceive the mystery that is waiting for them. Ultimately, the contemplative journey is about trusting and waiting. To design a contemplative retreat following a depth model, activities need to be planned that lead the retreatants slowly and gently away from the familiar and into the mysterious. There is no need to push and no need to rush.

There is really nowhere to go. Participants may come on retreat and simply practice waiting. Others, imagining the contemplative life as an ocean, may be ready to dive in. Others may wade in and wait there. Some may be swept to new places. The descent portion of the contemplative retreat looks like this:

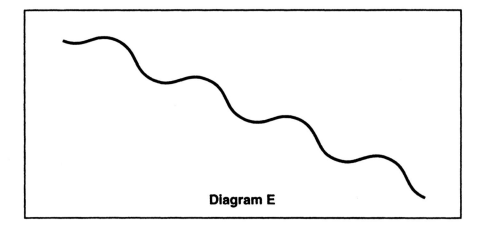

Diagram E

Activities introduced at the beginning of a contemplative retreat are designed to build trust and to practice waiting. They provide ways of experiencing the presence of God, of helping participants remember and know that God is with them. These activities, many of which are described in chapter 6, are activities from the kataphatic mode of spirituality.

The kataphatic tradition "makes generous use of metaphor and analogy in describing the mystery of God. It is concrete and incarnational, speaking of the divine by way of vivid imagery and storytelling."[1] The kataphatic path recognizes that we can understand and experience God through every aspect of creation. We hear God's call in the hoot of an owl. We see Christ looking at us through the eyes of a homeless woman. We feel God's love in the embrace of a friend or when the warm sun shines on our backs. With our minds we struggle to understand God through a passage from Scripture or a new theological idea or a poem. We use our imaginations to fashion prayers of intercession. We engage our memories to utter prayers of confession. We bend our knees in supplication and with our voices we sing hymns of praise. All these experiences are a part of the kataphatic path, and they "affirm God's relationship with creation and the possibility of knowing God in and through the created order."[2]

St. Augustine's definition of contemplation, which I described earlier, is in the kataphatic tradition: "The striving to understand those things that really and supremely are." The key words that place this statement within the kataphatic tradition are "striving," "understanding," and my additional word "experiencing." To acknowledge the fullness of contemplation and the entire shape of a contemplative retreat, we draw on the apophatic tradition in which the striving gives way to longing.

THE APOPHATIC WAY

The apophatic tradition takes us beneath our minds and imaginations, beneath our senses and our bodies, beneath our human relationships to a place of no thought, no images, no feelings—a place where we are stripped of all language and all knowing. "The apophatic heritage . . . stresses that no words, images, ideas, ideologies, or cultural expressions can gather up all that God is. Revelation brings us to mystery."[3]

A completely apophatic retreat invites participants into long periods of total silence. In addition to no speaking, participants are not allowed to read or write. The group gathers for long periods of silent meditation or prayer. Eye contact is not made between people, and physical contact is forbidden. Visual and auditory stimulation is kept to a minimum by very spartan surroundings, and food is kept purposefully simple and bland. This environment is designed to give participants the opportunity to relinquish language, "along with its powers of naming, entitling, and possessing. This leads, in turn, to the letting go of one's thoughts, the emptying of the self, and the act of loving in silent contemplation what cannot be rationally understood. . . ."[4]

On apophatic retreats in the Buddhist tradition, hard work and struggle are an integral part of the experience. People who attend such retreats believe that long and dedicated practice will ultimately lead to transformation.

A Buddhist retreat consists of a great deal of effort; even though Soto Zen speaks of "just sitting," a retreat means "just sitting" for thirteen hours a day, with a crack on the back as soon as your posture starts to slump. The idea is to break through our conditioning including the common notion that meditation, like anything else, is something you "do." Arduous practice of this sort soon makes it quite clear how little you can do; how little you are in control of the mind. It drives you to give up your ordinary assumptions about yourself and the world, so that something else can make its presence known. To discover this, you have to make the effort in the first place.[5]

In Christianity we embrace the concept and the experience of grace. Grace is that which we receive from the goodness of God. We neither earn nor deserve these blessings. They are given freely from the abundance of God's love. Therefore, on a Christian contemplative retreat, we rely more on grace than on effort. In fact, effort and striving can block the grace we are waiting for. "All we can do is to make ourselves available; to have an inner disposition that is receptive to the grace of God."[6]

DOING AND BEING

A Christian contemplative retreat can be either kataphatic or apophatic, for the reality of grace is experienced in both traditions. The retreats described in this book are more kataphatic than apophatic. Most Protestants who are trying contemplative retreats for the first time find the kataphatic way of retreat to be challenging. Putting God first, drawing God to the foreground of our attention is a new experience. Purely apophatic retreats would discourage many people from attending. A Christian contemplative retreat, however, is not complete if it does not point to the apophatic way. Including both traditions of spirituality, our contemplative retreat model now takes the following shape:

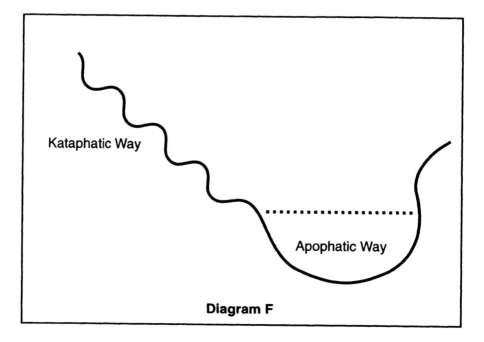

Diagram F

Kataphatic prayers and activities are introduced to help retreatants make themselves available to God. Silence prepares them for the possibility of being drawn beneath language. Community worship and individual prayer reassure participants that God is present and can be experienced in a variety of ways. As retreatants become more comfortable with silence and waiting, they may find themselves being guided and drawn into the apophatic way. This happens not by will power, not by effort, not by striving. "A mind not geared to productivity has the potential to receive revelation, insights, and graces that draw one into union with God."[7] The movement from the kataphatic to the apophatic cannot be programmed, manipulated, or forced. In the Christian tradition, descent into the apophatic comes as a gift from God.

Shaping a contemplative retreat to include the possibility of a shift from the kataphatic to the apophatic is not the same as designing the retreat with an apophatic experience as the goal. To set any spiritual experience as a goal for a retreat makes success or failure a distinct possibility. "I went on retreat for three days and felt no closer to God when I left than when I arrived," a retreatant could say with a feeling of failure. "I went on retreat for three days and melted into the abyss where my ego disappeared and all was pure light and love," a retreatant could say with pride and a feeling of success.

The purpose of a contemplative retreat is simply to attend to God. The retreatant does not fail or succeed; he or she simply practices attention for the duration of the retreat. We attend to God in any way that presents itself. We open ourselves to God's grace and receive it with gratitude in whatever form it appears. That grace may even be the absence of any experience of God, for the mystics teach that the absence of special feelings and insights of God's presence is where the mystery of God resides.

The kataphatic and apophatic traditions are not mutually exclusive. One is not better or more holy than the other. The traditions are interdependent and intertwined.

This intertwining is similar to melody and counterpoint in music. Both must sound if the fullness of the music is to be heard. Without the kataphatic emphasis, the apophatic way runs the risk of becoming contentless, separated from God's work in the Christ of history, and removed from the immediate needs of flesh-and-blood people. Without the apophatic way, the kataphatic has the danger of idolatry and confining God to our narrow ideas, concepts, and images.[8]

In order to intertwine the kataphatic and apophatic traditions in our understanding of contemplation, I will add to our statement in chapter 2. Our complete definition is: "Contemplation is the striving to understand and experience God, *and the longing to receive and embrace the mystery of God.*"

RETURNING

The way up from depths is as important as the way down the mountain. We cannot expect retreatants to simply return to the familiar and be ready for daily life. The length of the retreat will determine how much time to spend on the transition. Without prompting, retreatants begin to experience the tension of changing their focus from the interior to the exterior world. Some resist leaving, wishing to stay longer and to put off returning. Others are eager to go and pack their cars before the last session. One student pastor skipped the closing lunch and later told me, "I couldn't wait to get out of there! I turned my car stereo on full blast, opened my window, and let the wind tear at me. I grinned at all cars and the people and the busy-ness. I couldn't wait to get home to all the wonderful activities of my life."

I often use a reflection similar to the one the youth leader used with his campers. I ask people to remember who and what is waiting for them at home. I ask them to reflect on the people and activities they are eager to return to and those they are reluctant to encounter. Some retreatants are eager to talk about their retreat experiences when they get home. Others realize they have no words. Sometimes those who want to share have no opportunity to do so. One mother of teenagers knew she would not be greeted with three children eager to listen to her experiences. "They usually say something like, 'Where have you been?' 'Have you seen my red pants?' 'Do you know what my brother did while you were away?' 'Can I go to the movies?' 'What's for supper?'" We all laughed with her, knowing from experience most teenagers' lack of interest in their parents' discoveries.

A man spoke up, "My problem is the exact opposite. Our children are grown and gone, and my wife is very interested in this spiritual journey I am on. She will want to hear all about it, and I will have trouble finding words. She used to think I was withholding things from her, and she felt left out. Now she understands that it may take days before I am able to share."

People returning from a contemplative retreat are open and vulnerable. They have spent hours if not days in an interior landscape and have been protected from external demands. Because many retreatants have found a new sense of peace or gratitude or hope, they expect to carry that into their families and their workplaces and their neighborhoods. They are disappointed when they are not able to hold on to the retreat experience, and are surprised when they react more quickly with anger or frustration or tears than before they went on retreat.

"I walked into the house filled with gratitude for my family, took one look at the messy kitchen, and yelled at my kids," one young mother confessed. "The night I returned home," the retired electrician remembered, "the neighbor's dog barked until midnight. Before retreat I had actually gotten used to it. After retreat I was angry and began to fantasize about ways I could make the dog quiet."

Stepping off solid ground and sinking into the deep for an hour, a day, a weekend, or longer is about spending time with God. A contemplative retreat is a spiritual practice that allows us to practice the presence of God in all that we do and all that we are. Retreat time does not substitute for everyday life, but may give us new ways to approach daily living. When shaping a contemplative retreat, we must carefully attend to returning to our lives, for we are called by the psalmist to walk with the Lord "in the land of the living" (Ps. 27:13). This land includes our environment, our work, our family and friends, and neighbors near and far. This land draws us into relationship and action. As we deepen our understanding and experience of God during contemplative retreat time, we bring back to this land new ways of seeing and relating. In the poetic words of scholar and author Belden C. Lane, "Apophatic experience is never completed until it returns to kataphatic awareness and the exercise of compassion whose shape is justice."[9]

CHAPTER 4

LEADING A CONTEMPLATIVE RETREAT

The wise leader teaches more through being than through doing. The quality of one's silence conveys more than long speeches.

The Tao of Leadership

The students were listing the qualities of a good contemplative retreat leader.

"Gentle, accepting, and nonjudgmental," one student began.

"But clear and direct and well organized," added another.

"I think the good leader is more a facilitator who is able to step back and observe, who guides without manipulation, and who is basically unobtrusive," a United Methodist pastor shared thoughtfully. "The leader needs to trust the spiritual unfolding of the individual and the group."

"I agree," a Presbyterian laywoman concurred, "but the leader must also be confident and mature and able to step in and provide direction if things move off track. When I am on retreat, I need to know that someone is in charge."

"The good leader builds trust by being trustworthy and trusting the spirit," a retired pastor added to the discussion.

"We are all sounding so serious," another student laughed. "I think a contemplative retreat leader needs a fully active sense of humor. Contemplative retreats can be fun!"

"I want to add some more words," an Episcopal deacon said excitedly. "Compassionate. Gracious. Calm. Vibrant. Receptive. Challenging. . . ."

"Whoa! Slow down," another student interrupted. "This person is beginning to look like a saint!"

The group quieted, looking over the list of qualities they had generated. Then one student broke the silence.

"Contemplative retreat leaders don't have to be saints," she said. "They need to be contemplative."

Contemplatives are those who strive to understand and experience God and who long to receive and embrace the mystery of God. Contemplative leaders hold striving and longing first and foremost in their minds and hearts. Contemplative leadership flows from this place. When leadership comes from a contemplative heart, the leader watches for, listens to, and facilitates the things of God at work in the individual retreatants and in the group as a whole.

The qualities the students listed are important, as are the skills and techniques that follow; however, positive qualities, honed skills, and good techniques that do not originate in a contemplative life will not create true contemplative leadership. "The wise leader's ability does not rest on techniques or gimmicks or set exercises," writes John Heider, author of *The Tao of Leadership*. "The method of awareness-of-process applies to all people and all situations. The leader's personal state of consciousness creates a climate of openness. Center and ground give the leader stability, flexibility, and endurance. Because the leader sees clearly, the leader can shed light on others."[1]

Shedding light on others is at the heart of spiritual direction as well as at the heart of contemplative retreat leadership. In fact, spiritual directors and contemplative retreat leaders have many characteristics in common. The director and the leader both know the spirit of God to be the true director and leader. Both depend more on being than on doing. Both are about being present and compassionate. Both are connected to the stillness that knows that God is God. These ways of being flow naturally from the director's and the leader's spiritual disciplines and contemplative life. They can also be developed with leadership in mind.

DISCOVERING THE COMPASSIONATE OBSERVER

A compassionate observer[2] resides within each of us and is at the heart of all spiritual leadership. The compassionate observer is the part of ourself who sees the brokenness of others beneath their angry or disruptive or aggressive behavior; who knows the feelings of worthlessness or shame that lie within the braggart; who recognizes that both sides of a heated argument hold some truth. The compassionate observer sees and experiences the pain and suffering of another and weeps. The compassionate observer sees people and the world with the eyes of Christ. We are familiar with this place of compassion within us, but sometimes we have trouble finding it. We need a way to reconnect to what we most deeply know. The following exercise creates a path to the compassionate heart of Christ.

On one piece of paper write all the reasons why you would be a good contemplative retreat leader. List the skills that you think would be helpful, such as your organizational ability, your attention to detail, your knowledge of the Bible, your years practicing centering prayer, your experience with the Myers-Briggs Type Indicator. List the qualities you have that are congruent with contemplative retreat leadership such as hope, humor, maturity, wisdom. Do not worry whether something is a skill or a quality. Simply write down all you believe would make you a good leader. Pay attention to your feelings and thoughts as you write your list.

When you have completed the first list, take another piece of paper and begin to write down all the reasons you think you would not be a good contemplative retreat leader, such as your tendency to get overexcited, your forgetfulness, your pride, your need for control, your age, your grief, your impatience. Allow this list to grow even if you begin to feel uncomfortable. Pay attention to all your feelings and thoughts as you write this list.

Now put both lists before you on a table or a desk or the floor. Put some space between them so you have to turn your head to see first one list and then the other. Close your eyes, take a few deep breaths, and let go of the thoughts and feelings generated by the list making. As you breathe normally, imagine a flame of compassion within you, and let each inhalation give life to its warmth and light. With each exhalation, imagine you are breathing out judgment, intolerance, nonacceptance. After a few moments, turn in the direction of your first list.

Imagine possessing all those qualities and skills. Pay attention to the image of yourself: your physical posture, your facial expression, the way you move, your body at rest. Pay attention to your feelings and how your mind is working. Simply look at yourself with the eyes and heart of compassion. Then let the image fade.

Now turn in the direction of your second list and imagine yourself with all the qualities and lack of skills that would keep you from being a good retreat leader. Pay attention to this image of yourself: your physical posture, your facial expression, your ways of moving and resting. Look closely at your attitude and feelings and thoughts. Look at yourself with the eyes and heart of compassion. Simply look.

After a moment, bring back into your mind's eye the first image so you can see them both together. Is there anything you wish to say to either of them or to both of them together? Listen to your silent words to be sure they originate in compassion. If they do not, breathe in slowly, feeding the flame of compassion, then breathe out, letting go of judgment, and then look and speak again. When you feel complete, let the images fade and sit for a moment reflecting on what you have seen and felt. You may wish to write about the experience.

Although the details of this exercise vary from person to person, a common learning seems to occur. From the place of the compassionate observer, most people see the value in both images. Both parts of themselves have gifts to offer contemplative leadership. The gift of the first image is competence, an acknowledgment of experience and maturity. The gift of the second image is humility and the ability to know that the leader is not in control of the contemplative retreat, for the Spirit moves as and where it will. The leader in whom the first image is unchecked by the second is in danger of relying on his or her own skills and leaving no room for the Spirit to move. When the second image is unchecked by the first, the leader is in danger of passivity and abdication of responsibility.

When a leader becomes totally identified with either one of these polarities, true compassion is not available, and fluidity and presence to the moment are impossible. We all know the experience of being stuck. I remember a retreat I led at which one of the retreatants was a well-known spiritual director whom I greatly admired. All my feelings of inadequacy and worthlessness took over, and I felt paralyzed. Everything I did and said seemed not to be good enough, and the worse I felt about myself, the more absent to the group I became. I do not think anyone was aware of what was churning inside of me, but I knew I could not continue to lead the retreat from that place. During evening prayer I was graced with compassion for myself and for the other person. I saw what I was doing to myself and heard the voice of compassion say, "Just be who you are. That is enough." I saw that I was putting the other person on a pedestal, and I realized that this was not a comfortable place for her to be. I breathed a prayer of gratitude and was able to continue the retreat from a more balanced and compassionate place.

I also know the experience of being stuck in my competence. One time

I was so excited about a new activity I had designed for a retreat that I totally missed the retreatants' experience. Competently and clearly and decisively I led them through the exercise, and when they began to respond, their experience was nothing like what I had expected. Instead of opening to them and feeling the wonder of surprise, I decided they had done the activity incorrectly. I tried to lead them to my conclusions, but they would not cooperate. I left the session feeling frustrated, angry at their resistance, and disappointed that my great idea hadn't worked!

The compassionate observer can be active in other places of ministry besides retreat leadership. A pastor told me a story about missing a pastoral moment. "I was at a difficult church meeting regarding the budget," he said. "One of the committee members mentioned in passing that her beloved pet had died. I went right on with the business at hand." Later, in reflection, he remembered the moment and began to criticize himself for his insensitivity. Then he changed his attitude and looked at himself, the incident, and the grieving woman with compassion. With his heart open, he went to the phone and called her. "I expressed my sympathy and told her I knew what the loss of a pet can mean," he reported. "She wept in gratitude and told me a few stories about her animal. We both felt better after the call." This minister's compassionate observer led him away from judgment and straight to the heart of compassion for himself and for the woman. This shift guided him to compassionate action.

The compassionate observer is always available to us and lives between and beyond polarities. It beckons to us and waits for us, and when we are open to it, we know the joy of seeing and responding to ourselves and others from the compassionate heart. We never arrive there to stay, however, because the compassionate observer is not so much a place as a process. The process is one of paying attention to what is happening in ourselves and others and making choices with clarity of vision and compassionate hearts. When we do this, our work flows from the compassionate observer within us.

LEADING FROM COMPASSION

Leading from compassion must include compassion for ourselves as well as for the retreatants. Compassion for ourselves is not about selfishness, but rather comes from keen self-awareness. "True self-interest teaches selflessness," wrote Chinese philosopher Lao Tzu.[3] When we are aware of what is going on within us, we do not need energy to deny it or hide it. We see ourselves with compassion, which allows us to make a compassionate response.

Imagine that your retreat is beginning. The group is gathering after supper on the first night. You begin with an introduction of yourself, an orientation to the retreat facility, and an explanation of the retreat schedule. You speak about the need to honor confidentiality during the retreat and after the retreat. Then you ask people to reflect for a moment and then to tell the group briefly who they are and what they are looking for on this retreat. As people begin to share, one person comments on each person's response. He jumps in with a tale of his own, asks a clarifying question, or makes a connection to a Bible story. What do you do?

The first step is to become aware of what you are feeling. Are you angry? Annoyed? Sympathetic? Discouraged? Bored? However you are feeling, be compassionate with yourself. All these feelings are appropriate, and you now know how other members of the group are possibly feeling. They are waiting to see how you respond. If your response comes from compassion for yourself, for the overly active retreatant, and for the group, it will be kind and clear and will build a trusting community.

Group trust building is often believed to be about participants' getting to know and trust each other. Surely, that is part of it. But more important is participants' gaining trust in the leader. Will it be safe? Is there a plan? Is she compassionate? Is he open? Will my experience be honored? Are different opinions allowed? Retreatants learn this by watching and listening to you respond to them and to other group members. Therefore, the opening session of a retreat is of great importance.

Twenty minutes into the first gathering of a five-day retreat, a staff member of a large retreat facility burst into our room to say (in a very loud voice) that one of the retreatants had parked in the wrong place. The group fell silent. I was shocked and angry at the interruption. I knew I had to respond. With compassion for myself and for the man who was simply trying to do his job, I spoke softly, calling him by name: "Thank you, we will take care of it." He left satisfied. I felt the temptation to talk about him and his behavior with the group, but I resisted and returned to the activity in process.

After the retreat many of the retreatants mentioned to me that the way I handled that situation was instrumental in building trust. "I was so ready to talk about him and make him wrong," one person said, "but you didn't go there." "I was so annoyed," another said, "and you were so kind." "Your calm decisiveness was reassuring," added another. Although I felt many of their same feelings, my compassionate observer was alive within me and lighted the way to a compassionate response.

GROUP PROCESS

Although a contemplative presence and a compassionate observer are the keys to contemplative retreat leadership, there are some practical things a leader can do to build trust, provide safety, and invite individual exploration. The group needs to know that you are trustworthy and in charge, but that you are willing to let them go into their own journeys to follow the spirit in their own lives. A retreatant wrote about his retreat leader: "He gave us enough limits to keep us informed and plenty of freedom to explore. He gently led us, then let go of our hands, allowing us to find our own resources in our individual lives."

Offering this freedom and pointing retreatants toward their own experience can begin in the opening session. In addition to asking participants to share what they came for, I also ask them what gift they bring to this group. This reminds them that they are not only here to receive but to give. In recognizing and naming their gifts, they begin to take some responsibility for the community as well as for themselves. I ask them both questions at the same time, so if a retreatant launches into a long story about need, I can gently break in and ask: "And what gift do you bring to us?"

In the opening session I also have the participants share in groups of two or three as well as with the whole group. Even when the group is very small, I use this configuration because it takes the focus off me. While the groups share, I sit quietly, center myself and find my way to my compassionate observer. I establish a presence that is there but not involved in the details of their experience. At the very beginning of the retreat I am letting them go.

Small-group sharing also hones listening skills in the retreatants. They learn the importance of listening to others as well as to themselves and to me. Many people who come to a retreat are looking for a spiritual teacher, someone to guide them on their way. They often imagine the retreat leader will be that person. "The search for a teacher is really more a necessity to develop a 'listener' within us," writes Rabbi David Cooper. "Our work is not so much to find a teacher as to improve our own receptivity and sharpen our ability to hear the teachings all around us."[4]

Another way to develop the "listener" in each person is to set some guidelines for large-group sharing. You might say: "When you speak, speak to the center of the circle. The rest of us will simply listen, treating the words as an offering. We will not respond but simply accept what has been given." Allow people time and space to share. Sit comfortably in the silence between offerings. Adopt a position of "soft eyes," looking more at the center of the circle than at individuals. Gently remind people of the guidelines if they jump in with a response. Remind yourself not to comment on or teach off of what is being said. A quiet nod, a brief smile, a simple "thank you" holds the stillness of this sacred sharing.

"I went on a contemplative retreat where the opening session became a place for people to tell their life journeys," a student shared. "People were very emotional, and we got lost in each others' stories. How can a contemplative retreat leader prevent this from happening?" This slide into full personal disclosure, the desire to use the retreat as a support group, or the need to create drama can emerge at any time in a group. Participants need to understand that contemplative retreats are not about processing their every experience, insight, and feeling. "Endless drama in a group clouds consciousness," writes John Heider. "Too much noise overwhelms the senses. Continual input obscures genuine insight. Do not substitute sensationalism for learning."[5]

Clear questions with a specific focus can guide retreatants into appropriate sharing. "Why did you come on retreat?" can open more than you want to hear. "What specifically called you to this retreat?" will elicit a more contained answer. "How are you feeling about this experience?" may open a floodgate. "What did you learn from this experience?" will bring a more reflective response. Containing stories and emotions does not mean that retreatants do not share deeply and feel deeply on retreat. Tears are welcome, laughter is invited, despair and hopelessness are acknowledged. But these findings are not brought to the group to be encountered, encouraged, supported, or processed. They appear in the group because they are part of the retreatants' immediate experience.

The behavioral guidelines set by the leader at the beginning of the retreat and the clarity of the leader's questions and invitations usually prevent rambling disclosures. But there may be a retreatant who ignores signals, who does not understand what a contemplative retreat is about, or who is so needy that he or she begins to dominate the group with tales about his or her life. When it becomes clear that this is where the sharing is headed, the leader can calmly interrupt with a reflective comment such as, "I can see you are upset," "I realize this is difficult," or "You have certainly experienced much loss." Then invite the retreatant to close his or her eyes and breathe, deeply at first and then more regularly. When breathing is calm, offer a suggestion that guides the retreatant to another way of coping with the life situation besides spilling it out before the group. "You have a lot to bring to God during this retreat." "When the group session is complete, why don't you write or draw your experiences." "I think our Bible study will help you with your concerns." "We can talk more about this in spiritual direction."

On a contemplative retreat, group time is not about encountering one another or processing the retreat experience. Although some of this may happen naturally, and a certain amount of sharing is beneficial, the leader's task is to remind participants that the true focus of the retreat is their experience of God. Gently, the leader can shift any encounter or need to process into the spiritual dimension by reframing the retreatant's experience. If one retreatant is prone to give another advice, the leader might say: "Those are good ideas to be considered. Now she will need to take them into prayer, for ultimately the solution will emerge from her relationship with God." When a retreatant challenged me saying, "You aren't sharing enough. I want to know what you think and feel and believe." I responded gently, "This retreat is not about me. It is about you and your relationship to God."

Contemplative group process is ultimately about seeing with compassion, trusting, and letting go. John Heider summarizes:

> When you cannot see what is happening in a group, do not stare harder. Relax and look gently with your inner eye. When you do not understand what a person is saying, do not grasp for every word. Give up your efforts. Become silent inside and listen with your deepest self. To know what is happening, push less, open out and be aware. See without staring. Listen quietly rather than listening hard. Use intuition rather than trying to figure things out. The more you can let go of trying, the more open and receptive you become, the more easily you will know what is happening.[6]

ATTENTION TO DETAIL

Leading a contemplative retreat is about being a contemplative presence, leading from the compassionate observer, trusting the spirit at work in the individual and the group, and letting go of one's own agenda. This emphasis could lead some to believe that all the contemplative retreat leader needs to do is to show up, be compassionate, trust God, and see clearly what happens. There is an old Sufi saying that can offer us wisdom regarding this interpretation of the role of a contemplative leader: "Trust in God and tie your camel."

Surely the leader must ultimately trust in God. At the same time there are many details to attend to and loose ends to be tied up. Much of the work of leading a contemplative retreat is done long before the retreat begins. The following questions and suggestions may help you keep track of the planning process. You may discover that you need to decide these issues in a different sequence from the one I have written. Skip around all you wish, but make sure you have considered them all.

1. Where and when will you hold your retreat?

Many retreat houses schedule groups more than a year in advance. Do not plan a retreat and then go looking for a place. Visit the retreat site so that you know what is provided and what you will be responsible for. Find out which other groups are scheduled for the same time. It is difficult, but not impossible, to hold a contemplative retreat in the same space as a junior high youth camp.

Talk to the retreat house staff about how many rooms you will need, whether they are handicapped accessible, what provisions are made for special diets. Check to see if retreatants will have single rooms, double rooms, or whether the retreat facility offers only bunk rooms. This information will help you decide whether to use the facility and what to tell retreatants who are considering attending.

If you plan to hold the retreat in your own church, do the same kind of exploration. Decide which rooms you will use and how you will provide food. Check to see if any other activities are scheduled for that day. I once arrived to lead a retreat in a church where congregational pictures were being taken that day. Over a hundred people came and went during the morning. They were dressed up, excited, and glad to see friends. The festive air of that activity did not blend well with our silent retreat.

2.   What will be your retreat theme? How will you announce the retreat?

Chapters 5 and 6 provide many suggestions for retreat themes, activities, and schedules. Read those chapters, keeping in mind the purpose of the retreat and the people for whom it is intended, and design accordingly. When your theme and design are in place, decide how you will publicize the retreat. If it is only for members of your congregation, use the Sunday bulletin, the newsletter, and announcements at Sunday worship, committee meetings, and education classes. If you plan to make the retreat available to the wider community, you may wish to announce it in your denominational mailing or a local newspaper.

3.   Who are the retreatants?

One month before any retreat that will last more than two days, I ask participants to fill out a questionnaire designed to give me some information about themselves. I ask them about special needs they may have, and I inquire about their experiences with other contemplative retreats and what they are looking for on this particular retreat. I also ask if there is anything they would like for me to know about them. This question gives them the opportunity to share something about their personal lives if they wish. Their answers help me know what issues retreatants are struggling with, such as grief, career change, or an important decision that is coming up.

4.   What are your arrangements for food?

If a retreat house provides meals, find out what times they are served. Inform the staff about retreatants' special needs. If you are responsible for feeding retreatants, decide whether you will order out, ask for potluck, or give people an opportunity to leave the retreat to find their own lunch. Prepare a schedule so people can volunteer to be responsible for serving and cleaning up. Serving regular and decaffeinated coffee and tea, fresh fruit, juice, and simple breads creates an environment of hospitality when people gather in the morning. You will need to decide if and when the food will be available during the remainder of the day. One retreat leader reported how distracting it was to her and the group as people continually got up to fill their plates and then munched during guided meditation and the following sharing.

5.   What equipment will you need?

When the retreat house has been scheduled and a theme and plan are in place, you will need to attend to physical details. Will you be using a CD player? What tapes and CDs will you need? What about Bibles or hymnals for study and worship? Are there handouts you would like retreatants to read? Do you plan to have responsive readings available or prayer services printed? Will you need to have that done before you leave for retreat? Other supplies you may need are crayons and drawing paper, paper and pencils for people who forget their own, copies of the retreat schedule, sign-up sheets for some activities, bread and wine or grape juice for communion along with the cup and plate. I also like to have candles and matches for prayer spaces and a chime to begin and end silent time during worship services. Sacred objects and flowers or plants also help to create a sacred space in which to hold the retreat activities.

6. What will be the cost of the retreat?

You will want to make it affordable for those to whom you want to offer it. Will scholarships be available? Many retreat houses request a deposit when a reservation is made. Will the participants pay the church or the retreat facility directly? What are the financial arrangements if the event is cancelled?

7. Have you made arrangements for transportation?

Some people need rides, others enjoy offering rides, and still others find driving to and from a retreat alone to be part of the contemplative experience. Matching riders with willing drivers ahead of time is respectful of everyone's needs.

No matter how attentive you are to details, the unexpected will occur. I once got a flat tire on the way to a retreat I was leading. Another time a sudden storm blew in before the retreat ended, and we needed to leave immediately to avoid being snowed in. One retreat leader asked someone to pick up hymnals, and the person brought Bibles instead. Another reported that she arrived at retreat to discover she had forgotten her CD player. On one retreat a retreatant was taken ill during the night and needed to leave for medical care.

The purpose of careful planning is not to control the retreat or the retreatants, but to provide space so you can attend to the surprises that are an integral part of a contemplative retreat. "The leader of my first contemplative retreat was deliberate and organized, but not manipulative," a retreatant wrote. "He modeled what he was teaching and led us into experiences, so we could find the contemplative in ourselves. He handled the unexpected calmly and with gentle humor."

Paying attention to detail before a retreat does not set a rigid agenda and lock the leader into an immovable plan. Rather, with everything in place, both leader and retreatants have the safety and the freedom to follow the prompting of the Spirit. Careful planning removes the need for urgency, rushing, and scattered behavior during retreat time. If the leader is not trying to find the CD containing the evening's opening song five minutes before the prayer service begins, she can be present in the worship space, silently welcoming retreatants as they arrive for prayer. If the leader is not running around searching for matches, he can have the candle lighted as he waits for a retreatant to appear for spiritual direction. If the opening session is planned and schedules are ready to be handed out and the rules are clearly delineated, the leader can become silent inside and listen from his or her deepest self to the retreatants as they arrive. By attending to details, the leader is able to be a calm and prayerful presence, finding within himself or herself the stillness that is the foundation for contemplative leadership.

SELF-CARE

Retreat leadership is both energizing and tiring. It is a privilege and honor to be with people in prayer, to introduce them to new ways of attending to God, and to share their spiritual journeys. Retreat leadership feeds the soul. At the same time, retreat leadership is hard work. Just because it is spiritual work, do not assume it is easy. Being present to groups and individuals for long periods of time can be exhausting. Jack Kornfield, Buddhist monk and retreat leader, shared his own experience of fatigue in his book *Path with Heart*:

> In my first few years of leading retreats, I would find myself periodically overwhelmed. After three or four retreats in a row, with hundreds of individual interviews, I would gradually become drained, irritable with students and colleagues. At the worst there were days I felt burnt out and did not want to hear another student's problem. During this period I had the chance to see His Holiness Dujom Rinpoche for advice and instruction on my practice. I told him about this difficulty. . . . I hoped he would offer me a special visualization and mantra whereby I could surround myself with

light, recite sacred phrases, and be untouched by the intensity and path of seeing too many students and dealing with their problems. He asked for many details about how I practiced and taught, and then said, "Yes, I can help you." I waited for his higher . . . teaching, but then he said, "I recommend you teach shorter retreats and take longer vacations." This, I guess, is the higher teaching.[7]

In addition to the "higher teaching" of His Holiness, I have discovered some other important avenues to self-care. When possible I go to the retreat house a day early. I have time to get organized, do final planning, and take a mini, solitary retreat. If one day is not possible, I arrive long before the retreatants are due. After the retreat I allow time to reflect and pray about the experience. I carefully order my belongings so they are ready for the next retreat. When possible I schedule a day off after the retreat. I may have been away, but I have not been "on retreat."

I have learned to ask for help in planning and leading retreats. Because I am not musical, I often ask someone to assist with the music. Sometimes I will invite someone to attend and take responsibility for one part of the retreat program, such as teaching centering prayer or leading a session of morning yoga. I arrange for this assistance before the retreat. It is unfair to interrupt a retreatant's experience with a request for leadership help.

I sometimes ask for help in the initial stages of retreat planning. I may work with a retreat committee, inviting members' ideas for themes, schedules, and activities. I take responsibility for the final design, but creativity can be stimulated by interaction. When retreats are held in places where we are responsible for setting up the space, providing food, and cleaning up, I waive fees for volunteers. They attend the retreat for free and give a little of their time and energy. These volunteers may help with registration, serving food, cleaning up, and watching for any details that can make a retreat run more smoothly. I felt deep gratitude during a recent retreat when three volunteers quietly left the retreat at 11:30 A.M. to prepare lunch. I knew the meal would be ready at noon, which left me free to lead the retreat.

No matter how well you prepare for a contemplative retreat, the unexpected will happen and you will make mistakes. You may believe that you have thought of everything, only to realize you forget something important. You may be well grounded in your spiritual practices only to find yourself anxious and ungrounded during the retreat. You may discover that a certain retreatant tries your patience, and you find yourself inwardly judging and criticizing and entertaining uncharitable thoughts. You may realize after a session that you spoke too long and theoretically, lecturing instead of listening. You may remember making a comment to a retreatant or colleague that was not appropriate.

In other words, you will discover very quickly, if you stay awake to the process within, that you are not a saint. Your leadership will not be pure. You will make mistakes. But if you are a contemplative, you will be able to find your way back to your compassionate observer. You will remember that this retreat is not about you but about God's spirit at work in the world. You can also remember, as I do, the gentle question attributed to Rosemary Dougherty, co-director of the Shalem Institute: "Are you really so arrogant that you think that God cannot work around or even through your mistakes?"

CHAPTER 5

MODIFIED MONASTIC SCHEDULING

Lord—thine the day, and I the day's.

Dag Hammarskjold

In the middle of a silent, solitary retreat, I decided to live without clocks for 36 hours. At nine o'clock that night I took off my watch and put away the clocks. I read a while and went to bed. I awoke a few times during the night confused by not having any idea how long I had been asleep. Morning, when it finally arrived, was overcast and gray. I could not tell by the sunlight even an approximate hour.

My day became a series of fits and starts. I began to pray and my intention and focus would drift away. I kept asking myself if I was hungry, and I would prepare food I did not eat. I read aimlessly, never quite connecting to the written words. My journal beckoned, but I did not open it. I put off my daily walk and then was afraid to go out thinking it might get dark before I returned. Soon after dark I went to bed, although I was not tired. The night passed as I drifted in and out of sleep, anxiously awaiting dawn. As the first light appeared, I raced for my watch even though I knew it could not yet be nine o'clock. "It's 6:42!" I breathed to myself. "6:42!" With joy and relief I sank into a chair, wondering what had happened.

The week after my return from retreat, I discussed the experience with my spiritual director. "What was your intention?" he asked me.

"In my daily life I feel so bound by time, so controlled by it. Everything is scheduled and I believe I lose touch with my own rhythms. I thought that if I did not know what time it was, I would be able to pray as I felt called, eat when I was hungry, sleep when my body desired rest. I imagined I would read without having to say to myself, 'You have been reading now for two hours! Isn't it time to do something else?' I thought the absence of clocks would free me for deep concentration. But it was the opposite. I just oozed over the surface of things."

"What you did was rather silly," he said, smiling gently. "It goes against over a thousand years of monastic wisdom. Monastic life is ordered by specific times for prayer, work, study, and leisure. This structure does not restrict the monks and nuns; rather it frees them to live each part of the day fully."

Our continued conversation helped me understand why I felt so anxious and confused. He told me about group leaders who insist that participants check their watches at the door because it disorients them and makes them easier to control. We talked about creating schedules that provide space for deepening our relationship with God within boundaries. As a parent and teacher, I realized I knew that limits create true freedom but had never seen the parallel with retreat design. That experience and our ensuing conversations guided my study of monastic wisdom and my experiments with retreat schedules. The result of this endeavor is a contemplative retreat design that honors the monastic way.

CONTEMPLATIVE SCHEDULES

A contemplative retreat schedule[1] is spacious while providing structure by designating specific times for prayer, worship, meals, and other planned activities. A weekend retreat design might look like this:

Friday
4:00	arrival
6:00	dinner
7:00	orientation/opening session
9:00	evening prayers

Saturday
7:15	morning praise
8:00	breakfast
9:00	group session
12:00	lunch
4:30	Bible study

	6:00	dinner
	8:00	evening prayers
Sunday		
	7:15	morning praise
	8:00	breakfast
	10:30	closing session
	11:30	Communion
	12:00	lunch

I begin with a talking dinner, close with a talking lunch, and hold all the other meals in silence. With a small group I might provide spiritual direction on Saturday afternoon and Sunday morning for anyone who wishes to discuss his or her retreat experience.

All community activities begin on time but have flexible ending times. The Saturday morning group session may last an hour or longer depending on the group. When a schedule lists ending times, it looks and feels more rigid. Feel the difference in your own response if the Saturday morning schedule were presented in this style:

7:15 - 7:45	morning praise
8:00 - 8:30	breakfast
9:00 - 10:30	group session
10:30 - 12:00	open time
12:00 - 12:30	lunch
12:30 - 4:30	open time
4:30 - 5:15	Bible study

Even more rigid and less spacious was a retreat schedule I received in the mail. It was announced as a retreat for spiritual renewal, and each group session was given a topic. Although the topics were of interest to me, I felt a physical restriction simply reading the schedule and decided not to attend. What is your reaction as you read the schedule for that retreat?

	Friday	Saturday	Sunday
7:30		Morning praise	Morning praise
8:00		Breakfast	Breakfast
8:30		"	"
9:00		Group session	Group session
9:30		"	"
10:00		"	"
10:30		"	"
11:00		"	Worship/
11:30		Open time	Communion
12:00		Lunch	Lunch
12:30		"	"
1:00		Group session	Goodbye
1:30		"	
2:00		"	
2:30		"	
3:00		Faith sharing	
4:00	Arrival	groups	
4:30	"	"	
5:00	Opening worship	"	
5:30	"	Open time	
6:00	Dinner	Dinner	
6:30	"	"	
7:00	Group session	Group session	
7:30	"	"	
8:00	"	"	
8:30	"	Worship	
9:00	Good night	Good night	

Sometimes contemplative retreats are designed with more presentations than the weekend retreat I initially described. These retreats can still be spacious and open while following a fairly tight schedule. I usually preface the outlined schedule with a statement of purpose and an explanation of the group sessions:

> The purpose of this retreat is to draw closer to God. Together we will explore a variety of ways to pray and take time, alone and as a community, to practice opening ourselves to God. All six presentations will include experiential and interactive learning and an opportunity for silent reflection. Silence will be honored from evening prayers through morning praise.

The Many Ways We Pray

Day 1

7:30	breakfast
8:30	"The Experience of Prayer"
10:00	break
10:15	"New Ways to Pray"
12:00	lunch
	open time for personal prayer
3:30	"Listening to God"
5:30	dinner
7:00	"Praying with the Bible"
8:30	evening prayers

Day 2

7:00	morning praise
7:30	breakfast
8:30	"A Theology of Prayer"
10:00	break
10:15	"Intercessory Prayer"
11:30	closing prayer service

Another way to indicate the contemplative nature of a retreat is to describe activities as well as content in the retreat design. A one-day retreat might be presented as follows:

Discovering the Compassionate Heart

9:00	Gathering in song and gratitude
9:15	"The Experience of Compassion"
	Presentation
	Remembering, reflecting, sharing
	Dialogue
9:45	"Compassion for Ourselves"
	Guided meditation
	Silent reflection and prayer
10:30	Break
10:45	"The Prodigal Son/Daughter"
	Storytelling
	Presentation
	Dialogue
12:00	Lunch
1:00	"Compassion for Others"
	Presentation
	Silent reflection and prayer
2:00	Break
2:15	"Compassionate Outrage"
	Guided imagery
	Sharing
	Dialogue
3:15	Closing prayers

I design the schedule for a retreat very carefully, and I also realize it may not meet everyone's needs. I always tell retreatants that if the schedule does not fit for them, they are welcome to deviate from it at any time. Maybe they need to be alone rather than hear another presentation. Maybe they need to sleep instead of reflecting and journaling. Maybe they need to be outside when everyone else is inside, or be silent when everyone else is sharing. I encourage retreatants to study the schedule and understand its purpose and then to feel free to choose what will guide them more deeply into their relationship with God.

Designing Your Retreat

The Academy for Spiritual Formation, a program sponsored by an ecumenical ministry of the United Methodist Church, has developed a contemplative retreat design that is used in its programs throughout the United States. The five-day format engages two faculty presenters. One faculty person teaches each morning for an hour, after which the participants enter a full hour of silence for reflection and meditation. The group then joins together for 45 minutes of dialogue with the faculty person and each other. This rhythm is repeated in the afternoon with the second presenter. Included every day are prayer time, worship, and evening convenant groups during which participants share with five or six others their experiences, learnings, insights, and questions. Silence is honored after closing worship through morning prayers.

Occasionally a church decides to combine a contemplative retreat experience with many people's need for more active fellowship. When this is done, it is important to be very clear about the two intentions and the boundaries between them. One United Church of Christ congregation in northern Colorado has successfully blended contemplation and fellowship in its annual women's retreat.

On Friday evening the women gather for dinner and fellowship. After dinner they are guided by the retreat leader into an experience of centering and reflection, followed by evening prayers and the beginning of silence. Silence is maintained through morning prayers and breakfast. The group breaks silence in the morning session as they are again guided by the retreat leader into activities that help them attend to God. Periods of silence are an integral part of the day until five o'clock on Saturday afternoon when the women gather for an evening of socializing, which may include a movie, games, snacks, and plenty of laughter. The retreat ends Sunday morning with a service of worship that includes communion.

When designing your own retreat schedule, be creative and open to the movement of the Spirit. If your retreat design comes only from your mind and your will and the desire to "get it right," it can become rigid, even if it appears spacious and fluid. As you create the structure that allows retreatants to place themselves before God, watch for balance between silence and speech, between solitude and community. Remember that the monastic way includes worship, prayer, study, work, and leisure.

Work in a monastery often involves physical labor. The monks may tend the garden, cook for the community and guests, clean and repair buildings, feed and care for livestock, raise money, and respond to inquiries and reservation requests. For lay retreatants following a modified monastic schedule, work is usually the activity least attended to. If the retreat setting is such that the group does its own cooking and serving and cleaning up, work will easily become part of the schedule. When the retreat is held in a facility that takes care of all the retreatants' needs, I include work in two other ways. One is to translate work into physical activity such as walking, stretching, or movement. The other is to encourage retreatants to reflect prayerfully on their work lives. By bringing work issues on retreat, participants may discover the possibility of taking a contemplative attitude with them to the workplace.[2]

Leisure is another activity that may need attention. Many retreatants expect the whole retreat to be leisurely, and even though they have seen the schedule before they arrive, they are surprised at how rigorous a contemplative retreat can be. Arising early, praying, attending to the noise and voices that come in silence, and opening one's mind and heart to new ways of being with God all take energy and focus. I recommend short periods of light reading, handwork, picture puzzles, napping, or doing nothing. Retreatants often need a break from the intensity that can occur during contemplative time.

A question about what vowed members of a monastic community do for leisure came up on a visit to Christ in the Desert Monastery in Abiqui, New Mexico. A group from Ghost Ranch, a nearby Presbyterian conference center, had gone to the monastery to see the facility, participate in a liturgy, and learn about the monastic way. The brother who spoke to us was open and engaging and talked about the rhythm of monastic life. When he spoke about the period of leisure the monks enjoyed after their evening meal, one of the visitors blurted out, "What in the world do monks do for fun?" Without hesitating, and with a twinkle in his eye and a broad smile on his face, he responded, "We talk about the visitors!"

RETREAT RULES

In addition to outlining the schedule and expressing expectations such as keeping silence, beginning on time, and attending group gatherings, a retreat leader may establish other rules or be responsible for telling participants about retreat house rules. These rules may be about safety and involve candles, smoking, fireplaces, or woodstoves. Other rules may place restrictions on where retreatants can and cannot eat and drink, or where they can store personal food they may have brought for health reasons.

Many retreat leaders make rules about where talking can occur as well as when talking is allowed. "Many people who are new to contemplative retreats need to break silence," an experienced retreat leader shared. "So I provide a space where they can do that comfortably without impinging on the silence of others." You might designate a particular room for talking. You could ask for silence in the halls and the chapel and in the chairs immediately outside the retreat house. On retreats when rooms are shared, it is wise to make a strong plea for honoring silence in the sleeping rooms. "It's frustrating to look forward to silence," one retreatant lamented, "and then have to deal with a chatty roommate."

Schedules and rules often bring forth resistance in retreatants. Sometimes the resistance is expressed, but more often it is just below the level of awareness and festers in the minds and hearts and behavior of retreatants. Therefore, I find it useful to name the resistance they may experience and offer some ways to cope with it. One way is to remind them that following the schedule and the rules is not done to make themselves pleasing to God, for they are already and unconditionally loved by God. Following the rules is not done to please me or to make themselves into good or "holy" retreatants. Rather, obeying the demands of the contemplative retreat fosters an inner disposition and an availability to God.[3]

Rabbi David Cooper, author and retreat leader, offers additional wisdom on the topic of resistance and places the resistance in the context of the retreatants' spiritual lives. "Spiritual unfolding . . . requires a certain degree of surrender," he writes. "Thus the schedule, as an authority, provides a tension, constantly demanding surrender."[4] He also recognizes that instead of surrendering, "there are times when it is a good idea to break the rules all together. In this way we often discover how useful the rules are and how much breaking them interferes with the quieting process."[5]

This last statement affirms a decision I made as a retreat leader during a five-day retreat years ago. A small group of the retreatants were finding the silent meals difficult and almost impossible. They sat together and whispered and used hand signals at every opportunity. Others on retreat found their behavior disruptive and annoying. For the sake of the larger group, and out of compassion for their struggles, I offered them a place where they could take their food and eat and talk as they wished. They were very grateful and went off with delight.

One day later I noticed that one member of the small group had returned to the silent dining room and ate all her meals by herself. During spiritual direction she told me that she regretted going to the "talking room," because she had gotten into an argument with her friend and now that was all she was thinking about. The harsh words between them were in the foreground of her thoughts and prayers, and she was angry and anxious. "I wish I had never gone to that room," she cried. "I now understand the reason for limiting casual talk. If we had kept silent, none of this would have happened. I might even be discovering the stillness I so long for. Instead, I am all riled up."

Prayer and Worship

"A variety of prayer weaves through the monastic day," writes Paul Wilkes in his book *Beyond the Walls: Monastic Wisdom for Everyday Living.*[6] In addition to individual prayers and prayer time, community prayer and worship[7] is an integral part of a contemplative retreat and of a modified monastic schedule. "The simple prayers and the beautiful music helped me feel closer to God," a retreatant wrote. "I felt a sense of quiet community with the others who were experiencing the same closeness."

Some retreats begin with an opening worship service. I prefer to hold the first service of prayer or worship after we have joined in community in other ways, such as eating dinner together or participating in an orientation session or opening activity. I do this for two reasons. The first is practical, in that people coming on retreat do not always arrive on time. I believe it best for everyone to be together for the first worship experience. The second reason is that prayer can be experienced more deeply if people know with whom they are worshiping. If worship is the very first activity, participants are often distracted by wondering who the others are and what will be expected. When retreatants have had a chance to settle into their rooms, to greet old friends and be introduced to strangers, and to hear about the retreat content and process, they are more able to turn themselves over to God in prayer. Depending on the schedule, the first prayer service could be a liturgy before dinner, an evening prayer service, or morning praise.

Gathering for prayer first thing in the morning is the monastic way. I modify the monk's schedule so we do not pray at 3:00 A.M. (much to the participants' relief!) but wait until a time shortly before breakfast. On a retreat where everyone is familiar with the method of centering prayer, the morning prayer time may be one or two 20-minute sessions of centering prayer. On retreats where the prayer experiences of the participants vary, I prefer a simple morning praise service.

> Gathering music
> Opening words
> Praising God with our bodies
> Chant
> Psalm
> Silence
> Reading
> Silence
> Sending forth

The shape of the prayer service is the same as the shape of the contemplative retreat. In 30 minutes the words and music slowly invite the community down to that still place where they wait for and rest in the presence of God. Because the retreat day awaits them, I allow them to remain in that still place, using the sending forth only as a sign that the service is over. I repeat the opening words for the sending forth so the prayer that begins the retreatants' day also sends them forth into the morning.

When I open with "This is the day the Lord has made; let us be glad and rejoice in it" (Ps. 118:24), I end with "Let us go forth remembering that 'this is the day the Lord has made; let us rejoice and be glad in it.'" Another example would be this opening written by Rita Snowden of New Zealand: "I accept this new day as our gift, and I enter it now with eagerness; I open my senses to perceive you; I lend my energies to things of goodness and joy." To close the prayer service I would say: "Now, let us go forth, accepting this new day as our gift, entering it with eagerness; opening our senses to perceive God, and lending our energies to things of goodness and joy."[8]

After the opening I invite the community to stand to praise God with their bodies. We begin by planting our feet firmly on the floor with knees unlocked and do a series of gentle stretches. I ask them to move their heads in small gentle circles, first one way and then the other. I have them move their shoulders up and down and around, opening the upper parts of their bodies. I encourage them to gently let their heads fall forward with their chins on their chest and then slowly let their heads guide them down so their spines bend until their upper bodies hang forward from the waist. Their heads should be relaxed and their arms should hang limply. They do not bounce in this position; they simply hang, allowing gravity and their breathing to release tension. Then slowly they rise up, stacking one vertebra slowly on the next until they are upright and able to feel the energy moving in their bodies. Next, we focus on the arms, allowing them to slowly float upward until they are pointed to the sky. Then I invite them to stretch upward, one side at a time, as if they were picking apples off a tree. After stretching both sides two or three times, their arms float downward to be cupped in front of their hearts.

The time of stretching can be led in many ways. Practice morning stretching by yourself to discover what is comfortable and helpful for you. Then lead the group with your own words and your own reminders to "move gently," "feel the energy," and "don't forget to breathe." The purpose of gentle morning movement is to help retreatants attend to their bodies and to their breathing, and to feel the glory of being awake and alive.

The body meditation leads the group to a silent and physical form of intercessory prayer. This prayer consists of praying first for the world, then for others, and finally for ourselves. The wording can vary, and the focus of the prayer can change. Pray from your own longings, your own needs, your heart. To give you an idea of the rhythm of this intercession, I offer the following prayer:

Cup your hand lightly in front of your heart. Imagine you are holding the planet. Look carefully at the continents, the oceans, the high mountains, the valleys, the forests, the deserts, and the plains. Imagine all the peoples, some at peace, some at war, some in want, some in plenty. Imagine all God's creatures, the four-legged, the winged, those that crawl, and those that swim. Take a moment to attend to one part of God's creation for which you have special concerns. Then, breathing a silent prayer for creation, lift the planet slowly up, up, up into the loving presence of God, holding it there. Opening your hands, release the world into God's loving care to be loved as only God can love. Allow your hands to again be cupped before your heart.

Imagine you are holding all the people in your life. Your family and friends, the people you work with, the people of your congregation, the people here with you on retreat. Imagine the people who are near and dear to you, those with whom you are having difficulties, and those whom you often forget. Take a moment to attend to a few people for whom you have special concerns. Then, breathing a silent prayer for them and all the others, lift the people in your life slowly up, up, up into the loving presence of God, holding them there. Then release these people into God's loving care to be loved as only God can love. Slowly allow your hands to again be cupped before your heart.

Now imagine you are holding yourself. The self you were as an infant and child and adolescent. Your young adult self, the self you are today, and the one you are becoming. Imagine your feelings—your joy, your anger, your sorrow. Imagine your faith and your doubts, your questions and your insights. Imagine yourself at work, at play, at rest, at prayer. Take a moment to attend to a special concern in your life. Then, breathing a silent prayer, name yourself with your full name. Lift yourself slowly up, up, up into the loving presence of God, holding yourself there. Then release yourself into God's loving care to be loved as only God can love. Allow your hands to return to the place before your heart, and let all the people say: Amen.

The body meditation and prayer are followed by a chant. "Chanting is an integral part of the world's religious traditions," writes Brother David Steindl-Rast. "That is because at a certain pitch of religious experience, the heart just wants to sing; it breaks into song. Paradoxically, you could say when the silence finds its fullness, it comes to word."[9] Chanting in morning praise allows the silence of the night to break forth into song. As the many voices join in the repetitive phrases and blend in harmony, the retreatants feel their connections to one another and remember that they are in community before God.

After chanting, I read a psalm. Because silence is more important than the words in a contemplative prayer service, the readings are short and the silence long. I usually read only part of a psalm and then read some or all of it twice. I choose a prayer, a Scripture passage, or a poem for the second reading that seems appropriate for the group and the season. Each reading is followed by at least three minutes of silence, which is ended by the ringing of a chime.

Evening prayers are similar in structure to morning praise. I begin with a musical selection or a simple chant to gather people and focus attention. A reading comes next, with five minutes of silence following, ended by a chime.

I lead the group in spoken intercessory prayer after which we sing together the Taizé chant "O Lord Hear My Prayer." I close the service with a brief blessing that leads them into the stillness of night.

Some denominations have a liturgy for evening prayer that they prefer to use on retreat. Other denominations enjoy borrowing from our liturgical sisters and brothers to design a more formal prayer service than I have outlined. As you use, borrow, and create, keep in mind that the purpose of evening prayer is to bring the community together in praise of God and to send people forth with the assurance that they are held in God's love.

Many retreats end with a prayer service or a worship service that includes communion. Consider carefully what will best serve the community as an ending ritual. When I end a retreat with communion, I design the liturgy to be similar to the prayer services the retreatants have already experienced. Therefore we use chanting and readings and silence. I include a short Scripture passage from the New Testament and read it four times in the style of lectio divina (see chapter 6). Communion is simple, and when possible the members of the community serve each other around the altar. We end with sharing the peace of Christ and a benediction.

Just as prayer weaves through a monastic day, community prayer and worship weave together a contemplative retreat. Without communal prayer time, participants may get lost in ideas that have been presented or that they have encountered in their reading. They may begin to focus on the group, putting one another in the foreground of their minds and hearts. They may become isolated in their reflections and prayers, forgetting that they are a part of a larger whole. Coming together regularly for prayer and worship reminds retreatants that "where two or three are gathered in my name, I am there among them" (Matt. 18:20).

PRECIOUS TIME

Time seems to shift and slide on a contemplative retreat. Even with a schedule, hours may seem to pass in a moment, or minutes may feel like hours. Sometimes retreatants chafe at the need to be places on time, feeling that it restricts their freedom. They may find the routine confining and wonder at the daily, monthly, and yearly regularity of life in a monastery. They wonder how the monks survive.

Their routine may appear to be an exercise in deadening regularity, but in the monastery there is enough time for everything. Time is not considered a limited commodity; each moment is all the reality that anyone can hope to experience, and that moment is now. And now. And now.... Time in a monastery is shaped into a series of frames to experience God—in prayer, in work, in eating, sleeping, talking.... For only when time is understood as precious, but not scarce, do we begin to live.[10]

A modified monastic schedule introduces retreatants to the experience of precious time. In community prayer they do not need to decide whether there is enough time to pray. Prayer is all there is. During meals, they need not question whether or not to eat. Eating is all there is. When they gather for Bible study, they do not need to decide if they would rather read a novel, for the Bible is all there is. When they encounter open time, they know it as limited, precious, and enough. On a modified monastic schedule, retreatants experience the paradox of scheduled time, just as the monks do. "The Trappists laugh at time, bending it to their resolute wills by obeying it precisely."[11]

CHAPTER 6

THEMES, ACTIVITIES, AND SPIRITUAL PRACTICES

*Spiritual practice has no permanent goal
and is always introducing new challenges.*

Rabbi David Cooper

"Our church has decided to have a contemplative retreat," a local pastor called to tell me. "What shall we call it?" "Why not call it 'A Contemplative Retreat,'" I replied. He thought I was joking, but I was serious. "Don't we need a theme?" he asked. "Maybe a catchy title will attract more people."

When we name a retreat descriptively, with a title like Prayer Retreat, Silent Retreat, Contemplative Retreat, people know what they are signing up for and what to expect from their time away. A United Methodist conference in Texas sponsors an annual contemplative retreat called "A Day Apart." Descriptive titles help participants who are coming to any of these retreats know that God will be at the center of the retreat and that time will be structured and activities provided to open participants to the presence of God.

The theme of all contemplative retreats is God. How we attend to God may vary. On a centering prayer retreat, the primary way participants will attend to God will be through that form of prayer. A weekend called "Sounds of Silence" will use the practice of silence as the primary form of attention. A retreat title from the Bible might suggest participants will use Scripture as a means of attending to God.

If a retreat is not named descriptively, a title may be chosen from qualities, or fruits, of the Spirit such as compassion, hope, gratitude, stillness, peace. Other themes may grow out of topics of interest to the community, such as "Contemplation and Action," "Different Gifts, One Spirit," "Christian

Service." Many churches combine ideas, so a retreat may be announced as "Contemplative Retreat: Psalm 23" or "Diving In: A Contemplative Retreat for Men," "Prayer Retreat: The Practice of Intercessory Prayer," or "A Day Apart: Practicing the Presence of God."

Contemplative retreats may be directed toward a certain group of people. Many churches sponsor men's retreats and women's retreats. Some provide retreat experiences for those who are living with loss or for those who are primary caretakers of an ill or elderly family member. Retreats may be designed for groups that already exist within the church structure, such as the church boards, singles, or youth. If the idea of contemplative retreats is new to a congregation, the retreatants will need to be told what to expect. One way to teach people about contemplative retreats is to share a schedule or an outline of the day. Prospective retreatants will see on that schedule prayer and worship, periods of silence, Bible study, and other contemplative activities. Knowing what they will be doing and not doing lowers their anxiety and helps prepare their hearts and minds for a contemplative retreat.

Retreat themes and titles help focus the leader as well as the participants, for the theme guides the choice of the activities to be included in a retreat design. The following spiritual practices are ones I have included on different retreats. I am sure you are familiar with additional contemplative practices. All these activities serve the individual by teaching new ways to attend to God. They also serve the community by providing a focus for conversation when the group gathers for study and experiential learning. You will not be able to include all these activities in any one retreat. Choose the ones that best fit your retreat theme, your overall retreat design, and your personal leadership style.

TALKING ABOUT SILENCE

Before a group agrees to be in silence together for any length of time, a discussion about silence is wise. When retreatants are invited to speak of past experiences as well as their fears and hopes for the silent times, they are more likely to enter into the experience wholeheartedly. One way to begin the discussion is to ask the retreatants to respond briefly in writing to a series of questions. Some evocative questions are:

Were you ever silenced as a child? As an adolescent? As an adult?
Do you silence others today?

Has anyone ever used his or her silence to punish you?

Do you use your silence to punish others?

When has silence deepened a relationship?

Have you ever done a task in silence with another person or with
     a group?

Has group silence ever been frightening to you?

When do you experience silence as a gift?

Where and when do you long for more silence in your life?

What is the difference for you between silence alone and silence
     in a group?

Choose five or six of these questions or others from your own experience. After people have had a time to reflect and write, invite them to share in groups of two or three. The purpose of small-group sharing is to allow retreatants to give voice to their experiences and to practice listening with compassion to the experiences of others. Intentional sharing builds community, and people will later remember and accept how others may be feeling when silence is being honored in the group.

A general discussion may be facilitated in the full group by asking: "What did you just learn about silence?" The sharing then expands beyond the small group and continues community building. As part of this discussion, I usually speak for a few minutes about what I call "the etiquette of silence." I remind them that the purpose of silence is to open space and to discover stillness. When they have a simple need or a question, such as "Did you find my journal I left in the chapel?" or "Please pass the salt," speaking is appropriate. I also remind the retreatants that they will occasionally break silence without thinking. They might say, "Good morning!" or "Excuse me," or "What a beautiful day!" and they can be gentle with themselves and each other when they do. Keeping silence is not something at which we succeed or fail. Keeping silence is a practice for the purpose of finding the still point within that allows us to be present in new ways to God and each other.

A story is told about a monastery in which the monks developed a complicated system of hand movements. Through their hands they communicated regularly and rapidly without saying a word. The gesturing monks created a very noisy environment, although no words were ever spoken. They missed the whole point of silence because the call to stillness was ignored.

At the end of the large-group discussion I offer a gentle reminder that the choice to be silent is theirs. They are not entering silence because of another's decision but because of their own. When I pointed out at one retreat that retreatants had a choice about keeping silence, one group member responded, "This choice is exactly what makes the difference between this retreat and an awful silent retreat I went on five years ago." She went on to share that at that retreat the participants had gathered for their first session for the purpose of sharing their spiritual journeys. They shared deeply and began to form a close community. In the evening, after the last story had been told, the leader informed them that they were all to keep silence until after breakfast the next day.

"She told us we were not to speak a word about what we had said or heard. We were just to pray for one another. Then she dismissed us," the retreatant explained. "We were stunned and angry. And we rebelled. We gathered in each other's rooms and talked and talked—not about the wonderful stories, but about the leader. And then we felt guilty. No one slept much that night and the next day we were very resistant. I was glad we were able to go home after lunch." Those retreatants had not been told that group silence was to be part of the retreat. They had no time to prepare for it and no choice in the matter. Ultimately, they did have a choice, and they took the opportunity to defy the leader.

In a talking session after the first period of silence, it is useful to spend some time sharing about the experience of silence. What did they like about the silence? What was difficult? What did they not like? What could they do if they wished to speak and also wanted to respect another's choice to be silent? Expressing their concerns and pleasures and "mistakes" allows retreatants to enter other periods of silence with easier minds and hearts.

GUIDED MEDITATION

Guided meditation, often called guided imagery, is a quiet, group activity that is highly effective on contemplative retreats. The meditations help to relax the body, open the imagination, and provide retreatants with a focus for their solitary reflection and prayer. Guided meditations can be created for any retreat theme.

At a retreat entitled "Discovering the Compassionate Heart," I invited participants into a meditation on self-compassion. First, I guided them into relaxation by having them focus on their breathing, listening for sounds in the room, and letting go of any tight places in their bodies. As they shifted positions and settled down, I had them focus on their bodies exactly as they were that day. They were to attend to places of discomfort or dis-ease, as well as physical experiences that evoked pleasure or gratitude. Next, I asked them to focus on their feelings, feelings they brought with them and feelings that had emerged in the course of the retreat. They were to recognize their emotional states exactly as they were that day. Then I guided the same quality of attention to their thoughts, their questions and confusions and doubts, their creativity and insights and answers. They were to honor their minds exactly as they were that day. As they focused their attention, I invited them to simply experience themselves in the present moment.

After a long pause, I invited them to open their eyes, slowly stand up, and carefully turn around to face the chair in which they had been sitting. I asked them to allow the heart of compassion to open within them and to look at the image of themselves with the eyes and heart of compassion. I invited them to hold that compassionate gaze, seeing themselves as if for the first time. If they experienced judgment or criticism creeping into their gaze, they were to take a step to the side, indicating the choice they had to see themselves and all of life with critical or compassionate eyes. I invited them to see whether they needed to speak any words to themselves from the compassionate heart.

When they had completed the gazing and the interior words, I invited the retreatants to sit down again and to feel the love and compassion directed at them. If they were tempted to block the compassion or turn away, I suggested they gently breathe in the compassion and the words that were so freely offered. I encouraged them to sit receptively as long as they were able and then, when they were ready, to begin to turn their attention to the sounds in the room and the people around them. I reminded them to stay connected to the experience of offering and receiving compassion as they slowly opened their eyes. We remained in silence for 15 minutes, allowing everyone time and space to write and reflect and pray about the experience.

Guided meditation is best followed by silence and the opportunity to write or draw. This time can be followed by dyad or triad sharing and then whole-group sharing. On a longer retreat that has extended periods of silence, I prefer to have people leave the session in silence. In their quiet solitary time the retreatants can extend their writing and drawing and reflect on and pray about the experience. The next day I give them the opportunity to share not only the meditation but the reflections and prayers that the meditation stimulated.

Although books and tapes of guided meditations exist, I believe meditations need to come from the leader's ideas and experiences. If you do use another person's idea, change it to make it yours. You might substitute your own words or eliminate a section you believe to be extraneous. You could simplify it or expand it. Make the meditation your own, so that in leading it you speak from your heart.

A guided meditation that explores resistance may be helpful on contemplative retreats because there are things we sometimes resist: silence, attending to the present, the spiritual journey, the contemplative life, self nurture, prayer. In guiding these meditations, I usually introduce the idea with the words "interruption" or "block" rather than the word "resistance." Many people resist the idea of resistance! What might interrupt gratitude or prayer or simple presence to the moment? What blocks the impulse to social activism or the longing to hear God's call?

These meditations can be designed in a number of ways. Group members might be guided to imagine themselves at prayer and then imagine being interrupted at prayer. What is their image of the interruption? Retreatants have reported rich images such as a huge calendar, their three-year-old son, or a parent who has never believed in prayer. Sometimes retreatants receive an image of part of themselves that keeps them from prayer, such as a playful child, an exhausted worker, or a couch potato. Once the interruption is identified, the guided meditation continues, inviting a dialogue with the interruption to discover more about it. Where did it come from? What is it doing there? What does it want or need? The final part of the meditation is to ask the interruption to join in prayer and to pay attention to what happens.

Another form of a meditation on resistance is to have the retreatants begin their meditation by imagining a safe and neutral place, such as a meadow or a park. Invite them to discover a path that leads away from the safe place toward something new. You can let individuals imagine where the path leads, or you can provide them with a sign on the path that points to "the contemplative life," "silence and stillness," "self-nurture," or "wisdom."

Invite them to walk along the path, noticing their surroundings, when suddenly something appears to block their progress. In my experience, retreatants' images have included a policeman with a stop sign, a brick wall, a huge ditch, a snake, a multitude of people, a diamond necklace. As in the prayer imagery, the meditation continues with the invitation to engage the block in dialogue to discover what it is, what it wants, and what guidance it has to offer. When the traveler has heard and experienced all he or she can from the encounter, the meditation leads him or her back to the meadow or the park or to whatever safe place was initially created.

Retreatants are often surprised that during the meditation they are not guided through the obstacle to continue on their journeys; however, I designed these meditations to emphasize that God is in the meadow and God is also on the journey, as well as in the obstacle and in the interruption. Many people believe the spiritual life is about getting somewhere, that the sacred is elsewhere. I believe the spiritual life is being where we are. If the couch-potato part of me interrupts prayer, then it needs loving attention. If I cannot proceed on my journey because a wall blocks my path, I need to stop and discover what the wall has to offer.

The young mother with a three-year-old son realized that *he* was her spiritual practice now. She realized how her son and her longing for God could be integrated. She experienced God most easily in nature, and her son loved to go with her on her hikes. "Something lifted and lightened in that meditation," she said. "I realized I do not need to choose between my son and God."

The seminary student who was blocked on his way to the contemplative life by multitudes realized that his ministry would be among the people of his congregation. He came to understand that he would need to discover what it means to be a contemplative pastor. He realized he must not separate his contemplative longings from his active ministry.

If you decide to include guided meditation as part of your retreat, I offer the following guidelines:

1. Before you begin, explain guided meditation, its purpose, and how you lead it. Do not assume everyone is familiar with this particular spiritual practice.
2. Remind participants that the meditation is by invitation. They are free to follow your guidance, go where the spirit moves them, exit the meditation at any time, or go to sleep if they wish.
3. Guide them carefully into relaxation, giving them permission to keep their eyes open if they are more comfortable.
4. Use invitational language such as "If you are willing...," "I now invite...," "When you are ready...."
5. Keep the instructions simple, providing enough guidance to keep retreatants focused and enough openness to allow their imaginations full reign.

6. Speak slowly and clearly. Practice ahead with someone who can give you feedback, or speak into a tape recorder so you can monitor yourself.
7. Do not guide people in meditation by using the concept "down" (down to the bottom of the sea, down into caves, down into basements, down a spiraling staircase). Such imagery may bring up past memories that have been buried and forgotten.
8. Always bring the participants back to where they started in the imagery. Do not leave them in forests, churches, mountaintops, or on the road. Give them time in the imagery to reflect on their experiences. This serves as a transition back to the present time and place.
9. Invite them to come slowly back into the present by feeling their bodies on the chairs or floor, hearing the sounds around them, and slowly opening their eyes when they are ready.
10. Provide silence after the meditation for prayer, writing, or drawing.[1]

After guided imagery, drawing as well as writing helps people remain with their imaginations rather than immediately engaging their analytic minds. I provide an old box of crayons (hundreds of them, many broken and blunt) and large newsprint. Often retreatants are excited by the prospect of drawing and eagerly collect their supplies. Others are fearful and respond with "Oh, no!" or "I can't draw." Without insisting, I encourage them to try. I offer the suggestion of drawing with their nondominant hand. This gives them permission for the drawing to look like nothing and also connects them to the child within. Drawing is helpful in instances when a person does not get a clear image in the meditation and simply picks up a color and, with no object in mind, begins to draw. In this way the meditation continues.

Drawings can be used for sharing, for meditation during the retreat, and as a reminder of the retreat experience when participants return home. Images have the power to focus the mind and heart. I encourage retreatants to label and date their images and to look back at them as they might a journal.

PHYSICAL ACTIVITY

St. Paul said, "Do you not know that your body is a temple of the Holy Spirit within you . . . ; therefore glorify God in your body" (1 Cor. 6:19-20). To be faithful to Paul's command, loving attention to the body is part of a contemplative retreat. At the most basic level, simple nourishing food and comfortable safe shelter need to be provided. "I made the mistake one year of going on a solitary retreat in a remote campground," a young man reported. "I thought I could be with God in the midst of the beauty of creation. But I was so uncomfortable and so worried about my safety I was unable to simply be."

Besides basic nourishment and safety, retreatants can be guided into body awareness with very simple activities. Beginning group sessions and worship with a moment to focus on one's breathing brings awareness to our embodiment. Simple stretching can be taught and encouraged as part of retreatants' daily activity. If you practice yoga or some form of prayerful movement, you could lead the community in that activity.

Leadership of any physical activity needs to be gentle, sensitive, and invitational. Requiring everyone to dance on retreat is not a good idea! People may have issues of ability and disability that are rooted in the past as well as experienced in the present. Others worry about body image, and when asked to be physical in a group, find themselves feeling fear or shame or embarrassment.

If you are at ease with your own body and you incorporate some physical activity in your own spiritual practice, you may be comfortable guiding retreatants as a group. But do not assume everyone is as comfortable and as willing as you. If you are not comfortable with your own body, honor your limitations, but do not ignore the physical dimension of the retreat. Create ways to guide retreatants easily and gently into the sacredness of their embodiment.

A physical activity that everyone can do is to use their five senses to experience the Holy. Ask them to respond spontaneously, either in writing or verbally, to these questions: Where or when do you see the presence of God? Where or when do you hear the presence of God? Where or when do you feel the presence of God? Where or when do you smell the presence of God? Where or when do you taste the presence of God? You can substitute other phrases for "the presence of God" such as "the sacred" or "holiness" or "the spirit of God." The purpose of the activity is to help people see how their bodies can teach them about the holiness around them and how their bodies can attend to the presence of God.

Walking is another physical activity that can be encouraged on retreat. While walking, retreatants look for, listen for, feel the presence of God. Walking with all senses open to the presence of God is a contemplative practice.[2] Wandering through the grounds of a retreat house, walking around the block of an urban church, or even walking within the retreat setting involves body and soul in the retreat experience. If walking can be combined with the beauty of creation, retreatants find many ways to experience and attend to the presence of God.

"The most freeing part of the retreat were the long solitary walks on the paths that surround the retreat center," one retreatant reported. "They provided wonderful moments of sights, smells, and sounds. I felt enveloped by the holy." Two other retreatants—a married couple—took a silent walk together on a bright, clear winter afternoon. "Walking beside him, hearing only the crunch of our boots in the snow, I felt totally alone and fully connected. At the same moment we both looked up to see the dry snow dancing off the pine trees. The sparkle and the movement of light were unlike anything I had seen before. We stood together in wonder before the mystery of God."

Doing handwork and artwork can serve as other forms of physical prayer. One woman, a nurse with a long career, came on retreat with a heavy heart. Her relation with her only sister was difficult and at times oppressive. This relationship was the focus of her prayers and her journaling. She spoke about it in spiritual direction. She even dreamed about her sister, but the heaviness did not lift. On the final evening of the retreat, discouraged and disappointed, she picked up her embroidery. "I went to the living room," she told the group the next day, "with the attitude of 'I may as well get *something* done this weekend.' As I worked, attending to each color and each stitch, I was filled with a sense of peace, a lifting of the heaviness, and I saw clearly to the heart of my relationship with my sister. I understood what was happening. I knew what I had to do."

Many retreatants, once introduced to crayons, continue drawing during a retreat. They begin to include images in their journals, or they try sketching, or they create mandalas, which are sacred circular designs. One retreatant brought material to make collages. At the end of the retreat she shared her retreat experience through her creations. We sat in awe before the power of her images. No words were necessary.

"The body is your only home in the universe. It is your house of belonging in the world," wrote poet and philosopher John O'Donohue in his book *Anam Cara: A Book of Celtic Wisdom.* "It is a very sacred temple. To spend time before the mystery of your body brings you toward wisdom and holiness."[3] Ignoring our physical selves on a contemplative retreat, or in our daily lives, denies us the "home" God gave us and the opportunity to worship God with our bodies.

BIBLE STUDY

Lectio divina is a method of Bible study that is compatible with the purpose of a contemplative retreat. Lectio divina, which means sacred reading, invites the reader into the experience of the written text. Thinking about and studying the selected passage is part of the process, but not the end point. The purpose of lectio divina is to gently lead the reader to rest in God.

Many books on lectio divina are now available.[4] Each author brings a different interpretation to the ancient practice, but each teaches the same basic method. In its most fundamental form, lectio divina consists of four readings of the same short passage. Each reading is followed by two or three minutes of silence. The first reading (lectio) is to hear the passage as if for the first time and to listen for a particular word or phrase that touches the heart. The second reading (meditatio) gives the opportunity to think about the words of the text. The third reading (oratio) invites a response to God about the reflections. The fourth reading (contemplatio) gently leads the reader to rest in the presence of God. Recent writers have added a fifth reading (incarnatio) to move the reader's attention back to the world with the invitation to embody in life the word of God. An easy way to remember these steps is read, reflect, respond, rest, and return.

Reading the Bible in these four or five linear stages is called the scholastic method of lectio divina.

> This way of doing Lectio Divina developed in the Middle Ages at the beginning of the scholastic period with its tendency to compartmentalize the spiritual life. . . . The monastic form of Lectio Divina is a more ancient method and was practiced by the Mothers and the Fathers of the Desert and later in monasteries both East and West.[5]

The monastic method uses the same five experiences. But rather than being in linear form, they are placed around the circumference of a circle. They are "joined to each other in a horizontal and interrelated pattern as well as to the center, which is the Spirit of God speaking to us through the text and in our hearts."[6]

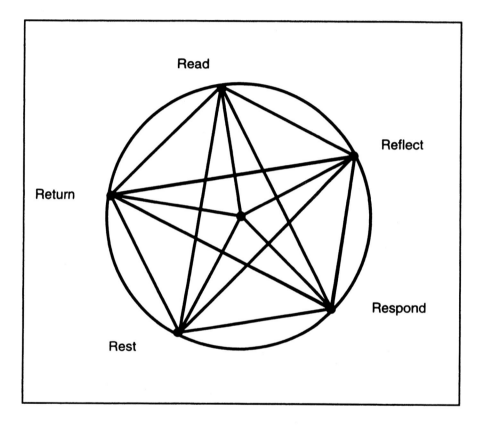

The monastic method of lectio divina allows the reader to be moved by the Spirit from one experience to another. This method is more accessible because retreatants do not need to figure out where they are and where they are to go next. It relieves them of having to do it "right." The monastic method also lends itself to group lectio divina, which includes discussion and sharing as well as periods of silence and rest.

The story of Mary and Martha (Luke 10:38-42) is an excellent passage for a group to use as a prayer focus during a contemplative retreat. One participant reads the story aloud from his or her Bible, while all listen for parts that touch their minds and hearts. As they follow the story in their own Bibles, they can also watch and listen for differences in translations. The variety of words makes the story richer than one translation can do alone. For example, in verse 41, Jesus tells Martha that she is "worried and distracted by many things" (New Revised Standard Version). In the King James Version she is "careful and troubled about many things." Martha is also said to be "anxious and troubled" (Revised Standard Version), "worried and bothered" (Phillips), and "fretting and fussing" (New English Bible). In The New Jerusalem Bible Jesus tells her "not to worry and fret about so many things," and in The Living Bible not to be "so upset over all these details." With all the translations taken together, we have a rich portrait of Martha, who is not only worried and distracted, but also careful, troubled, anxious, bothered, fretting, fussing, and upset. Most of us can identify with at least one of these words!

After the second reading, ask the participants what they know and feel about this passage. Some interesting questions might be:

1.   What is the relationship between Jesus and the sisters?
2.   Do you think that there are only the three of them in the house?
3.   What do you think was the usual behavior for women in Jesus' time?
4.   What do we know about Mary and Martha from other Gospel stories?
5.   Do you imagine that the way Mary and Martha relate in this story may have happened before?
6.   Which sister do you relate to more?
7.   Can each of us identify with both Mary and Martha?
8.   Do you think Jesus is being fair?

Remember, there are no right or wrong answers to these questions, and everyone's opinion is to be included. People may contradict each other or disagree. When that happens, the challenge is not to move into argument or debate, but rather to hear all the diverse ways that people relate to this passage. Sharing during lectio divina can be done in the form described in chapter 4. Ask the retreatants to place their ideas into the center of the circle where they will simply be seen and heard. The ideas are not to be picked up by another person for analysis or criticism or judgment. When a discussion is structured this way, more people feel free to offer their thoughts and feelings.

Participants can discover a deeper experience of the story when imagery and movement are integrated into lectio divina. Invite people into the story by imagining they are Mary and then imagining they are Martha. If they are able, retreatants can place their bodies into a position for each sister. As they assume the position of Mary, physically or in the imagination, invite them to experience themselves sitting at the feet of Jesus, listening to what he is saying. Pause and ask, "What is Jesus saying to you?" Then have them imagine Martha coming into the room, and imagine hearing her exchange with Jesus. Pause and then ask, "How do you feel about what is being said? What would you like to say to Martha?" Use your imagination to create more questions and more ways to help retreatants experience Mary in their hearts.

After Mary has been fully explored, have the retreatants shift to Martha by letting go of the body posture and the image of Mary and taking on the posture of Martha. Usually a startling difference is experienced in the body and then the feelings. Participants physically feel the differences between these two sisters. Ask them to imagine what Martha is thinking and feeling as she is busy in the kitchen and her sister is sitting at Jesus' feet. Ask them to imagine walking into the room and confronting Jesus and hearing his response to her. Have Martha hear the words that Mary might have spoken to her, and see if there is anything she would like to say in response.

After the guided imagery, participants may write or draw or share their new insights about this Bible story, themselves, and their relationship with God. To end the session, invite them to take this passage with them and to continue lectio divina with further reading, reflecting, and responding, and to allow the passage to rest in their hearts as the passage leads them to resting in the presence of God.

Other Bible passages for lectio divina might be the healing of the bent-over woman on the Sabbath (Luke 13:10-13), the healing of blind Bartameus (Mark 10:46-52) or the stories of the man who Jesus asks if he wants to be healed (John 5:2-9), the friend at midnight (Luke 11:5-8), or the lost coin (Luke 15:8-10). Choose a passage that relates to the theme of the retreat and one with which you are familiar and have prayed and lived before. Let your intuition guide you as you choose the scripture for a particular retreat and for the participants who attend.

At one retreat, I chose the parable of the lost coin, only to find out later that one of the participants had recently had a terrifying experience of being lost on a mountain trail. The imagery of the story allowed her to reframe her experience and discover a new understanding of what it could mean to be searched for by God. Another time I chose blind Bartameus after a number of retreatants had shared with me issues of "sight"—problems with both physical and metaphorical seeing. Sometimes I choose a scripture because it is alive for me in that moment, and I trust that it will become alive for the participants because of my enthusiasm.

A slightly different form of lectio divina comes to us from Martin Luther, who shared his understanding of prayer when his barber asked him for guidance.[7] Martin Luther instructed him to read a short passage from the Bible five times. The first time was to simply hear the words. The second time was to reflect on what teaching was present in the passage that needed attention. The third reading was to discover the gratitude the passage evoked. The fourth reading was to listen for the sin the passage reminded the reader of and to let the reflection lead toward confession. The final reading was for rest.

After using this form of lectio divina a number of times, I have shifted the order of the third and fourth readings so that confession comes before gratitude. I have found this sequence to more easily facilitate movement toward resting in God. This prayer form can be done silently or with some brief sharing. I often ask people to share in pairs their insights about the teaching, to stay silent during the recognition of sin and the confession, and then to share a simple expression of gratitude. When I use Martin Luther's form of lectio divina in worship, I follow each reading by one or two minutes of silence. I do not invite any sharing, but rather allow everyone to attend to the passage in their own hearts.

SPIRITUAL DIRECTION

Brief periods of individual spiritual direction may be offered during a contemplative retreat. Times can be made available for retreatants to sign up, if they wish. Any topic or issue is welcome in these sessions. I have had retreatants share dreams they have had while on retreat, issues they brought with them to retreat, deep grief or great joy that has been flooding them in the silence. Sometimes they come to see what spiritual direction is about.

The retreat leader is usually the one to offer spiritual direction, but that is not the only option.[8] Sometimes another spiritual director attends the retreat as a co-leader or as a staff person to assist with the spiritual direction. Whether retreatants come to spiritual direction or not, they like to know there is a time when they can talk with a compassionate listener if the need arises. The opportunity for spiritual direction increases the safety of the retreat.

A more informal way of handling the need for talking and compassionate listening is by providing the opportunity for retreatants to serve each other as spiritual friends. A sign-up sheet is offered with two spaces for names at specified times and places. If someone wishes to talk, they sign up and wait for another to write his or her name at the same time.

At the appointed hour the two meet to listen to one another. Because this is not intended to be a casual conversation, they decide who will speak first and who will listen. They might make the time sacred by taking a few minutes in silent or spoken prayer before they begin talking. The one not speaking listens compassionately and prayerfully and refrains from giving advice, or offering her or his own experience as guidance, or trying to make the other person feel better. He or she might ask a clarifying question, offer an image that comes to mind, or reframe what the person has said. When one person feels complete, they shift positions, have a few minutes of silence, and then repeat the process. They might close the session with a covenant of confidentiality and a final prayer.

Group spiritual direction is another way to provide retreatants with an opportunity to listen to one another prayerfully.[9] This model takes more time and is recommended for longer retreats when the group can meet two or three times. The model is highly structured and usually creates initial resistance. But as participants become familiar with the process, they understand the reason for the structure and the rules.

In each session of group spiritual direction there is one storyteller, three or four responders, one timekeeper, and at least one compassionate observer. Seven or eight people is an ideal number, but the model can be used effectively with up to 12. The participants arrange themselves in the configuration on the following page:

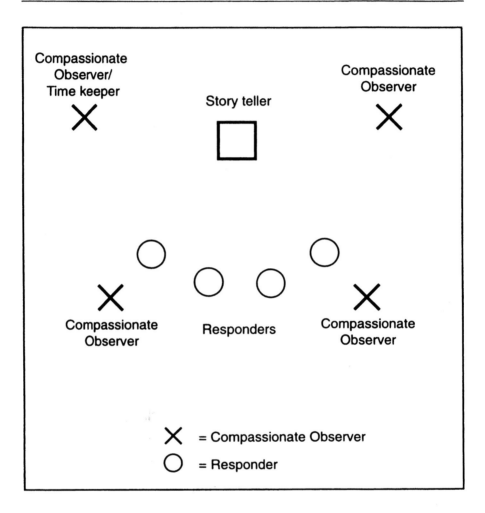

The time schedule is as follows:

Brief spoken prayer by the timekeeper
Storyteller speaks for up to 10 minutes and is given a two-minute
    warning after eight minutes if necessary
Silence for three minutes
Responders speak one at a time
Silence for three minutes
Storyteller may speak again
Silence for two minutes
Amen

In addition to the time schedule, a number of rules are an integral part of this contemplative process of group spiritual direction. While speaking, the storyteller is not interrupted by clarifying questions, words of sympathy, or any other verbal response. No words are spoken after the story and before the silence. After the silence has been honored, the responders briefly offer a response to what they heard in the story and in the silence under the story. They may reflect feelings: "I hear anger under your sorrow." They could connect the story to a Bible passage: "Your story reminds me of the passage in Paul's letter to the Romans (5:1-5) when he spoke of hope that is born of suffering." (This type of response can be given even if the exact chapter and verse is not remembered.) They could offer an image that came to them as they were listening and praying: "When you spoke about your sister, I saw the two of you on parallel paths, not close enough to touch but both of you going in the same direction." Responders are not to launch into their own experiences, offer advice, preach sermons, or try to fix the storyteller or the situation. The responders are not allowed to comment on or add to the other responders' offerings.

Compassionate observers pray silently for the persons speaking and listening in any way that feels right to them. The compassionate observers can practice listening and praying at the same time because they are not distracted by thinking about a response. In fact, they are not allowed to respond. After the session is complete, the content of the story is not to be spoken of again unless the storyteller chooses to bring it up with any member of the group. This rule provides strict confidentiality and protects the storyteller from well-meaning and sympathetic retreatants asking about the situation: "Was that Bible passage helpful? I thought of another one." "Did you and your sister resolve your conflict?" "I have been praying for you to find hope." "Are you working on your anger?"

Although the rules seem rigid at first, most storytellers in this process reflect how safe they feel, how important it is to have more than one response to their issue, and how they felt heard and seen and held in prayer. Responders are amazed how much more carefully they can listen when they have three minutes to reflect and pray before they respond. Many are relieved that the storyteller will have other ideas if their responses are not helpful. Some responders become aware of their competitive nature as they hope that their response was the best. Others recognize feelings of inadequacy if they think other responses were better than theirs.

Compassionate observers report the joy of simply listening with no expectation of responding. Many of them feel deeply about the story and the people involved, and they are free simply to feel the feelings. Tears of compassion are often shed by some or all during this process and connect participants to each other without words. One compassionate responder begged to be allowed to offer a reflection. "Her story is my story," she wept. "I need to tell her what helped me." When the group denied her request, she was angry, but she later reported with a rueful laugh that she understood the other woman could live her life quite well without her input. "This was a profound lesson in humility," she sighed.

Before you introduce group spiritual direction on a retreat, you need to participate in the process yourself in all the roles as many times as possible. You could find an existing group to join, or form one in your church. This contemplative model can be used in many settings other than retreats, such as vestry meetings, discernment groups, search committees, and book studies. Be creative in adapting it for your own needs and the needs of your congregation, but be very careful not to change the rules regarding silence and speech. My experience is that groups slide fairly quickly into discussion, including interruptions and cross talk and arguments. When this happens, the safety of the contemplative model is lost.

PRAYER FORMS AND SPIRITUAL PRACTICES

Going on retreat is in itself a spiritual practice. All parts of a retreat can become prayer when everything is done with the intention to understand, experience, and receive the mystery of God. In addition, a retreat can be a time to practice particular prayer forms or to learn about and begin spiritual practices that may be transferred from the retreat setting to daily life.

You can design a retreat around one prayer form or spiritual practice, such as "An Intercessory Prayer Retreat" or "A Journaling Retreat." A retreat might be designed to teach a variety of prayer forms or spiritual practices and could be entitled "The Many Ways We Pray" or "Spiritual Practices for Daily Living." On some retreats one prayer form is practiced by the community for the entire retreat. Participants might gather before breakfast for centering prayer or in the late afternoon for lectio divina. Some retreats also incorporate different prayer forms within the worship service using prayers of praise, confession, intercession, or gratitude.

In addition to these experiences of prayer, I usually invite retreatants to pray for each other during retreat. Their prayers of intercession can take any form they wish. Participants report that offering and receiving these silent prayers support and encourage them and help to build community. Many have continued these prayers for each other long after the retreat has ended.

Many books are available to help you decide which of these approaches may be best for a retreat in your congregation. The most comprehensive book is *Prayer: Finding the Heart's True Home* by Richard Foster in which he describes in detail 20 forms of prayer. Each chapter describes the prayer form and guidelines for practicing it and ends with a written prayer relating to the form explained. If you wish to practice centering prayer on retreat, you will find complete instructions in *Open Mind, Open Heart* by Thomas Keating. To explore intercessory prayer in depth, see my book *Praying for Friends and Enemies*.

Soul Feast: An Invitation to the Christian Spiritual Life by Marjorie J. Thompson and *Protestant Spiritual Exercises: Theology, History and Practice* by Joseph D. Driskill offer detailed instruction on a variety of spiritual practices. Both books have a chapter or section on developing a rule of life and on the prayer of examen, also called an examination of conscience. In addition, Thompson describes the spiritual practice of fasting, and Driskill includes a section on praying for a new earth and a section on journaling. For a complete resource on writing as a spiritual practice, refer to Ronald Klug's book *How to Keep a Spiritual Journal*.

DOING NOTHING

I was once told that a contemplative retreat needed three things: time to do something, time to do anything, and time to do nothing. The activities suggested in this book are for the time to do something. They also are options for individual retreatants when it is time to do anything. In addition, people on retreat need to be given permission and opportunity to do nothing. Someone may ask, "How does one do nothing?" The answers are paradoxical: "Do nothing that has meaning. Do nothing that has purpose. Do nothing that is hard. Do nothing that takes effort. Do nothing that is pleasurable or fun. To do nothing, do not strive or try or work or plan." So what do you do? An old friend of mine who taught kindergarten and would plan Saturday mornings to do nothing would only say, when pushed, "I play with my toes."

Learning how to do nothing is learning how to be. We know, after the fact, when we have done nothing for an hour or an afternoon or a day. Then we usually feel guilty. Doing nothing makes most of us very uneasy. We have been taught to do and produce and account for our time. A common question among family members and friends is "What did you do today?" Many people who come on retreat often have an agenda and the desire to accomplish something. Their hopes may be vague, but they want to go home having something to show for their time and money and effort.

Gerald May wrote in his book *Addiction and Grace*[10] that all of us crave time and space, but when we find it, we fill it up quickly because we are afraid of the spaciousness. We may fill the space with good and helpful and holy activities, but we are unable simply to be in the openness, receptive to the movement of the spirit. One retreatant recognized his compulsion to fill all his space with books. He called himself a "biblioholic." He reported, "I gave up this addiction for the duration of the retreat, which was very liberating for me. I let go of all my 'doing' and I received the gift of 'being.'"

To give retreatants the opportunity to receive the gift of being, retreat leaders need to choose among these many activities and practices the one or ones best suited for the retreat being planned. Making the choice is the retreat leader's spiritual practice. Too often, too many prayer forms and practices are included, because the leader did not have the discipline to let many of them go. Choose carefully from a prayerful mind and heart. When in doubt, exclude rather than include. Remember that on a contemplative retreat, less is more.

CHAPTER 7

FRUITS OF CONTEMPLATION

Only what is still can still the stillness of things.

Chung Tzu

People leave contemplative retreats with a variety of feelings and thoughts. Some feel enlivened and ready to return to their everyday lives. Others think they have just begun the process of quieting and are loath to leave, desiring more days of stillness. Sometimes retreatants do not know what they feel, thinking they might have missed something.

Often retreatants judge their experience and feel unhappy that they were not more disciplined, or that the retreat design did not include enough group work, or that they wasted their time sleeping, or that they got distracted by another participant's story. More often, retreatants will place positive judgments on the retreat. "It was wonderful! I feel so centered." "The chanting connected me to the heart of God." Retreat leaders also judge retreats and their own leadership. They criticize certain elements, take pride in the way a new activity went, are embarrassed when they think of the mangled audiotape during morning praise. Thomas Keating's advice about judging a period of centering prayer applies also to judging contemplative retreats: "The only way to judge this prayer is by its long-range fruits: whether in daily life you enjoy greater peace, humility, and charity."[1]

Church leaders need to keep these words in mind and heart as they evaluate the contemplative retreats they provide for their congregations and the effect these retreats have on congregational life. If we look for dramatic changes after one contemplative retreat, we will be disappointed. The work of the Spirit is done slowly and quietly and usually in secret.

First Congregational Church did not realize the fruits of the contemplative life until dissension threatened to divide the church and members discovered that their response to the conflict was different from in the past. Other churches will recognize the fruits of the contemplative life in other ways. In the stories that follow, people in congregations within other denominations add their voices to those of First Congregational Church to describe their experiences of transformation. Changes come slowly to persons and congregations. Fruit takes a long time to ripen. The task of churches that begin a program of contemplative retreats is to trust in the mysterious power of God to transform our individual and collective lives.

INTERIOR TRANSFORMATION

God is always at work in our lives. A contemplative retreat does not make that grace happen. But periods of contemplative reflection and prayer open us to the wonder of God's love and God's promptings. By going on retreat, we are in effect following the example of Mary and saying, "Here am I, the servant of the Lord; let it be with me according to your word" (Luke 1:38). Just as Mary could not have known what her obedience would ultimately mean, we do not know what our willingness to enter more deeply into relationship with God will mean in our lives. But we can trust that something will change, something will be different. "Yet we may not be able to describe the change because it takes place in the realm that is commonly called 'mystical.'"[2]

Months or even years after a retreat that introduced them to contemplative practices, people try to articulate what has been happening to them. "The people around me say I seem much more peaceful," one woman reported. "I'm not sure, but I think they see something I have not been aware of." "I am living my life more simply," a retired engineer wrote. "The change that began on retreat has continued gradually, almost without effort." "I realize I have more trust and assurance of God's loving presence in my life," said a woman living with much stress. "During times of anxiety I now welcome the discomfort as an opportunity to experience my aliveness and God's spirit deep within and all around me."

Many people recognized the growth of compassion for themselves and for others. "I have become more accepting of and more comfortable with my need for silence and stillness," an introverted man wrote. "I used to think there was something wrong with me." "I have let go of most of my perfectionist tendencies," a woman declared. "I am growing in my trust that God simply loves me." Another woman shared that before retreat she had been praying in a very limited and set way. "The time away opened me to many ways of prayer and has made me more intentional about spiritual growth."

"One of the unforeseen benefits of the retreat was that it helped me in my relationship with my wife," a young husband wrote. "We have had our differences, but in prayerful reflection I realized the profound connection that is at the heart of our marriage." Another man commented on his experience: "Practicing silence and developing the ability to listen has increased my ability to listen deeply to my own experiences and to the experiences of my family. I also find I am more willing to share myself with my friends and community." A single mother shared with me that after a number of contemplative retreats, her love seemed to flow more easily toward her children and the other people in her life. "I find myself just enjoying who they are and loving them for who they are. I'm simply feeling more love toward all people."

The compassion and love that grows through the contemplative life is often expressed by serving others. "My contemplative practices have helped me recognize and affirm my gifts," an active lay woman told me. "I appreciate and know how to create sacred spaces. In creating my own space for contemplation, I am inviting others to do the same. This is the quiet gift I give my church." Mary Hulst, senior pastor of Calvary Baptist Church in Denver, Colorado, believes that contemplation and mission go together. "We have always been a mission-minded congregation," she said. "We are in the top five churches in our American Baptist denomination in what we give in mission." The church's emphasis on social outreach is balanced by a strong contemplative program. Calvary Baptist hosts a monthly Taizé service, holds regular retreats, and offers classes and sermons on prayer. Mary quoted Elton Trueblood to describe the balance Calvary Baptist has achieved: "A life of service without devotion is rootless and a life of devotion without service is fruitless."

CREATING COMMUNITY

Silence by itself does not build community. Silence can produce fear, anxiety, isolation, and sadness. But silence experienced with others for a common purpose makes connections and creates bonds that can grow into community. "When you go on retreat with someone, you have one thing in common: you both believe in the contemplative dimension of the Christian life," a retreatant said. "Something is drawing us both to God. If we are authentically drawn to God, we are authentically drawn to one another."

For years I have been part of a community that gathers to sweat our prayers. We come together to dance and move in ways that help us discover the connection of body and soul. Our movement leads us to profound stillness and deep prayer. We share very little verbally. I know a few of the dancers' first names and practically nothing about their lives. Recently I bumped into a member of the community at a party. We were very surprised, because we did not know we had these friends in common. We threw our arms around each other and hugged, exchanged only a few words, and then parted. "Who was that?" my husband asked me later. "Barbara," I responded. "We dance together." I had told him all I knew.

A friend wrote to me, sharing that she had witnessed her husband rush across a street to greet someone like a long-lost friend. It turned out that the person was someone who went on the same annual three-day silent retreat. "They hardly speak more than two minutes at the very beginning and end of the retreat," she told me. "But they are real soul mates."

A young woman who attends contemplative retreats regularly described the development of community in terms of loss of ego. "One of the gifts of contemplation is that the ego moves to the back. With egos in the backseat, you are going to have a much more harmonious, compassionate community. The more people involved in contemplative activities means more egos taking backseats instead of jumping to the front." This psychological language corresponds to Thomas Keating's spiritual language that the fruits of retreat are peace, humility, and charity.

Mary Hulst believes that the whole church community is affected by the contemplative programs. Calvary Baptist creates programs for a diverse congregation. People have many options to choose from, and not everyone is involved in the contemplative activities; however, Mary says she finds it fascinating that the whole congregation takes pride in the ministry, even if they do not participate in it. "I think because our contemplative programs are ecumenical (and lots of Baptist churches are not ecumenical in nature), this congregation is drawn together in support of our contemplative ministry."

Contemplative programs often create community beyond the congregation that offers them. People from other Christian denominations and other religious traditions often attend Taizé services. I have friends who are Sufi who tell me: "The language is not of my tradition, but the spirit cuts across religious lines. The readings, the chanting, the prayers, the silence all nurture our souls." Contemplative programs also reach out to the unchurched. "Some of my friends would never accompany me to a Sunday service," a member at First Congregational Church in Colorado Springs told me, "but they willingly join me to walk the labyrinth." Calvary Baptist has community promotion in the newspapers for some of its retreats. Many people attend from the wider community as well as from within their own congregation.

Contemplation also connects people beyond our churches and our community, for the language of contemplation is universal. "As we examine the language of the mystics, we soon discover themes that are not limited to a single tradition—and indeed, studies have revealed cross-fertilization,"[3] writes Rabbi David Cooper. He also shares that when he retreats alone in silence, he experiences his connection to all those across time and space who have chosen to strive for and long for the things of God.

> Each moment of the day, thousands, perhaps tens of thousands, are sitting in strong concentration, deepening awareness not only for themselves but for everyone. We are opening our hearts, alone but all-one, joining others throughout the centuries in timeless realms. We dwell in unknown realities, hearing the whisper of universal truth, singing a song of the revelation of the divine.[4]

CONTEMPLATIVE LEADERSHIP

Church leaders, both ordained and lay, who follow a contemplative path have a profound effect on the individual members of their congregations and on congregational life as a whole. Not only are they well positioned to lead prayer groups, teach classes on prayer, organize contemplative worship, and direct retreats, but their own spiritual practice and interior transformation will affect their entire ministry.

Gene Yelken, a retired United Methodist pastor, met the contemplative life unexpectedly toward the end of his active ministry. He attended a church conference at which a workshop was offered on spiritual formation. "I had no idea what that was," he told me, "but I was curious, so I went to the session. The leader talked about the contemplative life for a half an hour, played some centering music, and guided us into silence. My life was changed. I had never known this form of prayer life was available to Protestants." Gene followed his discovery by seeking out retreats, learning to read the Bible in the form of lectio divina, selecting a spiritual director, and practicing solitary quiet times in nature.

He invited resource people to his church to lead contemplative retreats, which were well attended. While no one in the congregation took responsibility for the development of a contemplative program, Gene feels that his own contemplative practices had a subtle effect on his congregation. "I think that when one enters into the contemplative dimensions of life, that consciously and unconsciously something happens to everything you do—pastoral care, administration, preaching. I think that is because I was being fed as well as feeding. Many church leaders get so involved in giving that we don't take time to receive. My contemplative practices fed my soul."

Kelby Cotton, a Christian Church (Disciples of Christ) minister, entered the ministry as a contemplative. "I have told every parish I have gone to that before they hire me they have to know that I need two hours of prayer a day, one day of prayer a month, and one week of prayer a year. This is non-negotiable." Some churches thought he was trying to get extra time off, but they soon understood the authenticity of his request. In one rural parish many members of the congregation began to join him on his day of prayer. Some would take part or all of the day away from work. Others would pray at home or on their tractors as they did their chores. "I have always been open about how much I pray and how I pray. This is not a type of false humility, but rather an educational tool to help the parish."

In addition to being open about his contemplative practices, Kelby actively teaches his congregations how to pray. He teaches them in Sunday school classes, in sermons, one on one. "They can't escape prayer in this congregation," Kelby laughed. "I slip it in everywhere." He has introduced longer and longer periods of silence into Sunday worship: "At first the congregation couldn't stand it. Now, when silence starts I hear a collective sigh, see fists unclench, feel breath deepen. This congregation has come to love the silent prayers."

Kelby now serves an inner-city parish with a strong outreach program. It provides a street league for the neighborhood kids and a substance-abuse ministry, in addition to ministries that address the many needs within the congregation. "I always tie prayer to the work we are doing on the streets," Kelby told me. "I encourage people to take their prayer practice with them into their ministries. Many times they find themselves praying without even realizing it." With contemplative practice supporting the social action of the church, Kelby is seeing less burnout among those who serve. He smiled. "It's what I call the incarnational effect of prayer."

Leaders of congregations who take prayer seriously in their own lives are more able to design and offer contemplative programs that sometimes seem foreign to the Protestant tradition. "Protestants threw away too many things during the Reformation," mused Mary Hulst, "and contemplative practices were among them. I think it's been a good thing for a church like ours to hold on to something that many Baptist churches frown upon and feel is spooky and off-the-wall. Our programs have opened up the world of contemplative prayer to our congregation and to the wider community. Contemplative prayer is routine around here. It's expected. It's the norm. It's understood."

THE CONTEMPLATIVE CHURCH

The contemplative church is a church in the process of opening more and more to the spirit at work in individuals, the congregation, and the institution. A contemplative church does not give up its traditional programs, but allows the spirit to be at work within them. A contemplative church does not turn its back on the needs of the community and the world, but allows the spirit to guide them into the world. A contemplative church is not without conflict, but allows the spirit to assist in reconciliation and healing.

A contemplative church is not created by its programs alone. A regular schedule of retreats, active prayer groups, healing services, prayer days, and vigils all contribute to the church's growth in contemplation. But if the programs are only a horizontal add-on to the already existing activities of the church, you do not have a contemplative church; you simply have a busier church.

A contemplative church lives out of a vertical model in which God, the things of God, and the mystery of God are at the heart and soul of the church. I imagine that most people in most churches would say, "Of course! This church is about God and the things of God. That is why we exist." A contemplative church, however, does not only speak these words. It creates programs that actively support individual and congregational striving to understand and experience God and members' longing to embrace the mystery of God. A contemplative church looks like this:

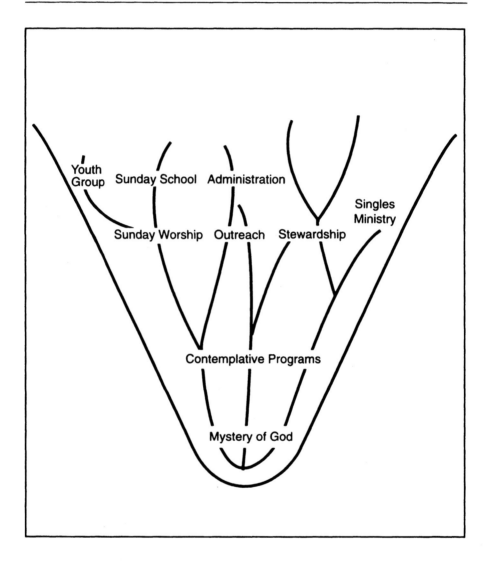

In a contemplative church, people are encouraged to turn to God for love and support and inspiration. People are taught to value their personal relationship with God and to make time to strengthen that relationship. People are given the opportunity to speak of things of the spirit and to use the language of the mystics. People are guided away from the world to experience silence and discover stillness. From the silence and stillness people are led back, to love and serve each other and the world.

The contemplative church is not only the body of Christ but the soul of

Christ as well. The contemplative church's soul shines forth for all to see. It draws people toward it and sends people out with love. The contemplative church stands as a witness to and a reminder of Jesus' last words to his disciples in the Gospel of Matthew: "And remember, I am with you always, to the end of the age" (Matt. 28:20).

HOME RETREAT WEEK

M any individuals design their own retreat time at home. They set aside a morning to read Scripture. They go to a city park for silence and solitude. They take one day and turn off the phones, do no chores, and use their home as a retreat house. That which we do at home to turn our attention to God is sometimes thought of as prayer practices or Sabbath moments rather than retreats. By any name, the individual is choosing to put God in the foreground of mind and heart.

In contrast, a home retreat week is designed so that members of a congregation can be on retreat at the same time, without going away together. The following structure for a home retreat week was introduced to me by Sylvia High Karlsson, a United Church of Christ clergy woman who first experienced it at the Mercy Center in Burlingame, California, during a month of spiritual director training. The first year that Sylvia offered a home retreat week in Denver, six people participated. The second year the number tripled. Participants discovered ways of attending to God during the week, ways to continue their attention beyond their retreat, and experienced the fellowship of shared spiritual practice.

Spiritual direction is at the core of this retreat week. Experienced spiritual directors from the community volunteer their time during the week to meet individually with retreatants. The director of home retreat week matches the spiritual directors with the retreatants, and they arrange their own schedule of meetings. The expectation is to meet every day for five days.

In addition to the meeting with a spiritual director, retreatants agree to do something each day to nourish their spiritual lives. The director may suggest the activity, or the retreatant may come to the week with an idea already in mind. During the week retreatants have the opportunity to talk about their responses to the activity, any resistance that may come up about doing it, or any graces they may receive.

This retreat design allows church members to retreat together in a spiritual sense even though they are not together physically. The congregation is invited to pray for the retreatants, and the retreatants are encouraged to pray for each other. "The knowledge that others are praying and supporting a person in retreat has intrinsic value for each retreatant," wrote Sylvia. The intercessory prayers also have value for the congregation as they add to the creation of a contemplative community.[1]

Community is also created among the spiritual directors who come together midweek for a period of group supervision. This time gives the directors an opportunity to raise questions and concerns about the process of spiritual direction with their particular directee. Directors disguise the details of the situation to honor the confidentiality of the directee. "This session was invaluable to me," wrote one director. "It introduced me to a model of group supervision,[2] and I was able to meet and talk with others engaged in the ministry of spiritual direction."

Organizing the home retreat week is the task of the retreat director. He or she needs to find and enlist spiritual directors for the week, interview them as to their qualifications, and discover enough about their training and spiritual direction style to match them with directees. The retreat director also finds ways to inform and invite participation from the congregation. Home retreat week can be announced in Sunday school classes and from the pulpit. Sylvia also found the church newsletter and Sunday bulletin good places for an announcement, such as the following:

Home Retreat Week

Have you ever been curious about going on retreat?
Would you like to do it, but time and responsibilities
seem to get in the way?
Are you seeking a deeper relationship with God?
"Go on retreat without going away on retreat!"
Here's how it works five days in a row:

* Meet with a spiritual director for one hour each
  day. You arrange a mutually convenient time and place.
* Spiritual directors for the retreat have received training.

You will be given a name when you sign up for the
retreat.
* Besides meeting with a spiritual director, you are asked to
do something intentional each day to nourish your spirit
like: take a walk, sit in the chapel, pray, hike, read, exercise, stare out the window, or do whatever is nourishing to
you.
* No fee.

Interested? Want more information? Give us a call.

With retreatants signed up, the retreat director matches spiritual
directors with directees, providing names and phone numbers. The retreatant
is responsible for contacting the spiritual director. When meeting times have
been established for the week, the spiritual directors contact the retreat
director, who arranges meeting places for the sessions. Spiritual direction
takes place in the church unless another place is more convenient for both
the directee and the director.

The retreat director is also responsible for setting a time for group
supervision and arranging for someone to lead the session. All directors need
to be notified of the meeting time and place. The director also needs to be
available during the retreat week to answer questions, discuss arrangements,
and handle the unexpected, such as a missed appointment or unhappiness
with the spiritual director/directee match. With all arrangements in place, the
director of home retreat week is called to be a contemplative presence, a
compassionate observer, and to trust that the spirit will work as it will in the
lives of the retreatants, the directors, and the congregation as a whole.

This model is not the only way to structure a home retreat week. Small
covenant groups could meet daily rather than holding sessions of spiritual
direction. People who sign up for the retreat could be matched as prayer
partners during the week. People could simply agree to do something
nurturing for their souls every day of the week and then to come together on
the final day for a brief period of sharing and a closing prayer service.

Be creative with the idea of home retreats, looking at the specific needs
and resources of your congregation. If you believe your congregation is not
a large enough to support a home retreat week alone, consider organizing it
together with three or four other congregations. You could work within your
denomination or connect with churches of other denominations in your

geographical area. Whatever you decide, remember that the purpose of home retreat week is not only to nurture the spiritual growth of individuals but to enjoy the community that can be established when people join together to attend to the presence of God in their lives.

RESOURCES

SPIRITUAL GROWTH

Among the many books designed for spiritual development, I have selected the following titles. Each book holds a particular message for religious leaders who are pursuing the contemplative life. May you find among and within them food for your soul.

D'Arcy, Paula. *Gift of the Red Bird: A Spiritual Encounter.* New York: Crossroad, 1996.

Paula D'Arcy is a writer, retreat and workshop leader, and psychotherapist who became exhausted and ill from overwork. This is the story of her healing and her discovery that she is like the African violet on her windowsill. "If I don't water it, it will die. I see that my spirit is not different. I am beginning to listen a lot. The silence is my water."

Griffin, Emilie. *Wilderness Time: A Guide for Spiritual Retreat.* San Francisco: HarperSanFrancisco, 1997.

For readers who are new to the practice of spiritual retreats, this book provides encouragement and practical suggestions for making space and designing your own solitary retreat. The experiences that this book will guide you into will give you the foundation for leading others on retreat.

Heider, John. *The Tao of Leadership.* Atlanta: Humanics New Age, 1985.

John Heider has adapted Lao Tzu's *Tao Te Ching* for modern readers seeking guidance in the ways of wise leadership. The book contains 81 short teachings for leaders of groups. They all easily translate to the leadership of contemplative retreats. "Good leadership," writes Heider, "consists of doing less and being more."

Hinson, E. Glen. *Spiritual Preparation for Christian Leadership.* Nashville: Upper Room Books, 1999.

"The central concern of a Christian leader should be . . . an intimate personal relationship with God," writes Hinson. He places this concern in an historical and contemporary context and provides the reader with information on time management and maintaining balance in everyday life. Three chapters are devoted to sustaining the spiritual life.

Muller, Wayne. *Sabbath: Restoring the Sacred Rhythm of Rest.* New York: Bantam Books, 1999.

The tradition of Sabbath creates an oasis of sacred time within a life of relentless activity. Muller teaches the reader how to create special times of rest and renewal in the midst of busy lives. He presents stories and practical suggestions in the context of the biblical and historical tradition of Sabbath.

Peterson, Eugene H. *The Contemplative Pastor: Returning to the Art of Spiritual Direction.* Dallas: Word Publishing, 1989.

Eugene Peterson places the art of spiritual direction at the heart of his pastoral ministry. With poetry and anecdote and sound scholarship he shares his own experiences in ministry. He gives permission and encouragement to put God first, to become "unbusy," and to cultivate humility.

Rice, Howard. *The Pastor as Spiritual Guide.* Nashville: Upper Room Books, 1998.

Spiritual guidance serves as the organizing principle for ministry in Rice's book. His chapters include "Worship as Spiritual Guidance," "Social Change as Spiritual Guidance," "Management as Spiritual Guidance," and "The Pastor as Person: Keeping Our Souls Alive."

Wuellner, Flora Slosson. *Feed My Shepherds: Spiritual Healing and Renewal for Those in Christian Leadership.* Nashville: Upper Room Books, 1998.

Wuellner knows from her own experience that Christian leadership can be overwhelmingly demanding, potentially wounding, and very stressful. Through the Gospel stories of the resurrection, the author offers hope and healing through the promise of the living Christ to be with us always.

PRAYERS

Keay, Kathy, ed. *Laughter, Silence and Shouting: An Anthology of Women's Prayers*. London: Harper Collins Publishers, 1994.

The authors of these prayers are women of history, women of different cultures, and women of today. Although all the writers are women, their prayers speak to the needs and joys and longings of men as well. Over 160 prayers are presented in categories such as "Who Am I?" "Other People, Other Places," "Work," "Justice and Peace," and "Ages and Stages." I particularly appreciate the brevity of most of these prayers. Much is said in very few words.

Klug, Lyn, ed. *Soul Weavings: A Gathering of Women's Prayers*. Minneapolis: Augsburg, 1996.

These rich, strong prayers reflect the needs and experiences of women and men of all ages. They are gathered from historic and contemporary women of faith from around the world. The prayers are arranged according to themes such as "We Are Not Alone," "Go Out with Good Courage," and "I Will Give You Rest."

Klug, Lyn, ed. *All Will Be Well: A Gathering of Healing Prayers*. Minneapolis: Augsburg, 1998.

This unusual collection of prayers addresses many areas of woundedness and healing. Many people who go on retreat are seeking healing in some aspect of their lives. This book offers prayers for physical healing, emotional healing, and healing of communities. It includes prayers for forgiveness, for compassion, and for gratitude. Of particular interest is the section entitled "Healing and Stillness."

Law, Philip, ed. *A Time to Pray: 365 Classic Prayers to Help You through the Year*. Nashville: Dimensions for Living, 1998.

"We can use these prayers to enter into a stillness that is vibrant with the Presence . . . ," David Adam writes in his forward to this collection of prayers. The prayers are arranged by month and by historic periods such as "Praying with the Early Christians," "Praying with Medieval Christians," and "Praying with Contemporary Christians." Law also has months devoted to Celts, saints and mystics, poets, and hymn writers. This collection draws the reader into a deep connection with the Christian tradition of prayer.

Loder, Ted. *Guerrillas of Grace: Prayers for the Battle.* Philadelphia: Innisfree Press, Inc., 1984.

"Prayer is one way of attempting to focus on grace, to pay attention to it, to praise it," Loder writes in his introduction. His written prayers help readers focus their attention on issues of the heart and issues of the world. He presents his prayers in sections, three of which are entitled "Quietness & Listening," "Comfort & Reassurance," and "Commitment & Change." For a contemplative retreat, some of his prayers may be too long, but many of them, and parts of some of them, are useful.

Merrill, Nan C. *Psalms for Praying: An Invitation to Wholeness.* New York: Continuum, 1998.

Nan Merrill has reworked the book of Psalms to make it more accessible for modern prayer. The prayers are addressed to Beloved, and help the reader connect more deeply to an all-loving and compassionate God. She intends the book to be in dialogue with the historical psalms of the Hebrew Bible. She hopes that it will "serve as an invitation to listen to the Voice of Silence that speaks within your own soul."

Mitchell, Stephen. *A Book of Psalms: Selected and Adapted from the Hebrew.* New York: Harper Collins Publishers, 1993.

Stephen Mitchell presents 50 psalms from the Hebrew Bible in a fresh and innovative style. Some translations are fairly traditional, but he does take liberties with the original text to make the prayers more accessible to today's readers. Although the poems are not rendered in inclusive language, I have found that many of his paraphrases speak to the soul.

Roberts, Elizabeth and Elias Amidon, eds. *Earth Prayers from Around the World.* San Francisco: HarperSanFrancisco, 1991, and *Life Prayers from Around the World.* San Francisco: HarperSanFrancisco, 1996.

Each of these books contains 365 blessings, poems, affirmations, and invocations from people throughout history and from many countries. Although only a few are from the Christian tradition, they all speak eloquently to universal human longing to be in relationship with the earth, with each other, and to the Holy. Many of them are quite short and serve well as a gateway into silence and contemplation.

MUSIC

Arnold, Kirk, composer/performer. *Just Like a Little Child.* Mountain Luv Publishing, BMI, 1997. Produced by Lone Wolf Records, 230 Randolph Avenue, Elkins, WV, 26241. Information: Kirk Arnold, Love Light Music, P.O. Box 1385, Florence, KY 41022.

The title song begins a cappella with the well-known children's prayer, "Now I Lay Me Down to Sleep," and continues with the question, "Where is the child who once prayed that prayer?" Individual pieces are upbeat and singable, with backup vocals and lyrics included. Orchestration is simple: piano, percussion, rhythm guitar, electric guitar, bass, and synthesizer. Several very inspirational songs are included, such as "I Need to Be Still and Let God Love Me" and "Help Me Forgive Them."

Bates, Isabella, producer, and Mark Huffman, recording engineer. *Sound Faith: Chants Used at the Shalem Institute.* Isabella Bates, 2303 Chain Bridge Road, N.W., Washington, D.C. 20016.

These simple chants can be used to call retreatants into session (as in "Come holy one be with us") or to aid them in ending a retreat (as in "God guide us home, Christ make us one, Holy Spirit flow, Love will be done.") Side 1 begins with the simple Eastern-inspired chant, "Om ah hum," which is chanted over one note of the scale within an easy range. Participants are exposed to the sensation of absorbing vibrations and are invited to sit quietly using a relaxed breath flow. Of particular interest is "Holy," which is a continuous two-syllable chant that is sustained by participants' staggered breathing, which allows them to enter and drop out at will. Eventually a chord is formed, achieving the effect of a beautiful, tranquil dissonance. All chants are easily within participants' grasp at first exposure.

Berthier, Jacques, composer, and Jerry Threadgold, musical director. *Laudate: Music of Taizé.* Veritas Productions, CC11, Lr Abbey St., Dublin 1, Ireland. Reproduced by permission of the Taizé Community, 71520, Taizé, France.

This music was recorded live, in English, at Evening Prayer and Prayer around the Cross at Gort Muire in an atmosphere of prayer. This is appropriate to use in prayer groups, worship services, or more formal liturgies. Included are reflective pieces for stillness as well as celebratory songs for festive occasions. "Stay Here" is introduced by a solo voice a cappella, followed by voices with melody and harmony, and later joined alternately by violin and soprano obligato. It lasts about 10 minutes. Although longer than the other chants, it is crafted like the others in that retreatants can easily join in. This recording is excellent for use in many types of liturgies as well as those in the style of Taizé, in which chants are interspersed with psalms, prayers, and periods of silence.

Doan, Lorraine, composer, and Sean McCleery, arranger/conductor. *The Promise.* Digital Audio DIDX 062628. Lorraine M. Doan Publishing, P.O. Box 413, New Hope, PA 18938, (215) 862-2014, FAX (215) 862-6966. (E-mail address is lmdoan@voicenet.com.)

Grand piano, acoustic guitar, and electric piano combine successfully to simulate an orchestral quality in this album of well-known classics and new works. Lyrics to original songs are included, but not sung, on this instrumental album. Sheet music is available and recommended, since matching lyrics to the unfamiliar melodic lines using only this accompaniment is difficult. Especially beautiful are the arrangements of such classic works as Johann Sebastian Bach's "Ave Maria," and "Jesu, Joy of Man's Desiring," Johann Pachelbel's "Canon in D," and Lorraine Doan's original, "A Lullaby for Corey."

Gentile, Norma, soloist. *Meditation Chants of Hildegard von Bingen.* Ave Maria Press. (ISBN: 0-87793-894-6) Notre Dame, IN 46556.

Norma Gentile manages to make the difficulty of calm execution and performance of unaccompanied voice sound simple. These 11 Gregorian chants of Hildegard von Bingen are excellent for retreat use. They are musically intriguing with great variation of tone, volume, and range and are set with only a short time lapse between numbers, making them appropriate for uninterrupted meditation. Gentile has an ethereal style that captures the essence of von Bingen's music, making *Meditation Chants* effective for the renewal of body and spirit. A German mystic, von Bingen founded two monasteries; wrote books on medicine, spirituality, biology, botany, and saints' lives; and composed over 70 Gregorian chants with Latin texts.

Halpern, Steven. *Music for Sound Healing.* Steven Halpern's Inner Peace Music: 1999 Open Channel Sound (BMI). SRXD 7878. (Website is http://www.stevenhalpern.com.)

Specifically avoiding the powerful effect of both rhythm and Western harmonic patterns, this work is designed to awaken inner awareness with quiet sounds and unfamiliar melodies. Thirteen tracks, each very different, convey a slightly different feel with varying combinations of grand piano, electric piano, choir, gently sustained string ensemble, harp, violin, and silver flutes. Included is one familiar piece, Johann Pachelbel's "Canon in D," so smoothly arranged that it is not immediately recognizable. One piece is reminiscent of Native American tonalities, another of the Eastern five-tone scale system.

James, Michael, violin/mandolin; Steven C. Warner, six- and twelve-string acoustic guitars, dulcimer, Celtic harp; and Craig Watz, acoustic three-quarter bass. *Commonsong Acoustic Meditations: Instrumentalists of the Notre Dame Folk Choir.* Modern Cassette Library, 0-87793-832-6, Ave Maria Press, Inc., Notre Dame, IN 46556.

Excellent musicians turn these old folk tunes into masterful art works. "Blind Man Shepherd," based on two Early American folk melodies, is significant in that the gently throbbing sound of dulcimer accompaniment under guitar and violin melodic lines resolves into a lovely, rhythmic pattern. Included in the album is music from Ireland, Appalachia, the Netherlands, and one Native American Dakota Odowan tune.

Talbott, John Michael, composer, and Phil Perkins, orchestration. *Come to the Quiet.* BWC 2019 MCA Distributing Corporation, 70 Universal City Plaza, Universal City, CA 91608.

This album of rephrased Psalms 95, 63, 51, 86, 23, 62, 91, and 131 is beautifully arranged and sung by Talbott, accompanied by full orchestra. The solo voice is often in duet with solo cello, flute, violin, or oboe. Each psalm exemplifies a different psalm type: assurance, supplication, call to worship, trust in God, or protection. Included are two works that are biblically based: "Peter's Canticle," a composite from 1 Peter, and "Phillipians' Canticle" from Phillipians 2:1-11. Also included is a beautiful rendition of "The Prayer of St. Francis."

Talbott, John Michael, composer, and Phil Perkins, arranger/conductor. *Table of Plenty.* TDC 4624 Troubador for the Lord, Music Services, Inc., Franklin, TN 37064.

Composed in response to liturgical reform emanating from Vatican II, this album is scripturally based. Perkins has arranged both familiar and less well-known pieces from many composers for full orchestra, choir, piano, acoustic and electric guitar, bass, flute, recorder, tin whistle, uillean pipes, Irish flute, didgeridoo, fiddle, hammer dulcimer, cello, and percussion. Rich and beautifully performed, the album includes three pieces appropriate for communion and quite immediately singable. Modern favorites, "Here I Am, Lord" by David Schutte and "On Eagle's Wings" by Michael Joncas, are exquisite, yet arranged simply. "Holy Darkness" is very appropriate for evening retreat services.

Warner, Steven C., director, and Karen Schneider-Kirner, assistant director. *The Seven Signs: Music to Celebrate the Sacraments.* (ISBN: 0-937690-71-6) 1999 World Library Publications, division of J.S. Paluch Company, Inc. 3825 N. Willow Road, Schiller Park, IL 60176.

This work celebrates in song the seven sacraments: baptism, confirmation, eucharist, ordination, funerals, anointing of the sick, and reconciliation. The songs are arranged for the University of Notre Dame Choir, cello, flute, classical guitar, percussion, piano, violin, clarinet, and oboe. The final piece, "Be Still, and Know That I Am God," is performed with full ensemble and soloist, and a simple response can be sung by retreatants along with the tape.

RETREAT FACILITIES

For retreat facilities in your area contact denominational headquarters. They will have a list of retreat houses and camps sponsored by their denomination. Many facilities are open to groups from other denominations as well as their own. Catholic retreat houses often welcome ecumenical groups. You can get their names from Catholic Diocesan Offices. In addition, you might wish to consult the following printed and on-line resources:

Jones, Timothy. *A Place for God: A Guide to Spiritual Retreats and Retreat Churches.* New York: Doubleday, 2000.

Two hundred fifty-seven retreat centers in the United States and Canada are listed and fully described in this new resource for spiritual seekers. In addition, Jones begins the book with a number of chapters devoted to reasons to go on retreat, how to prepare for a retreat, and what to do on retreat. Paul Wilkes wrote of this book: "A most helpful primer that alleviates anxieties and points out the redeeming, refreshing possibilities of going to ne of these spiritual havens."

Kelly, Jack, and Marcia Kelly. *Sanctuaries: The Complete United States—A Guide to Lodgings in Monasteries, Abbeys, and Retreats.* 1st ed. New York: Bell Tower, 1996.

This volume features 127 places the Kellys have visited that provide the time, space, and conditions for the mind and heart to come to stillness. In addition, there are over 1000 listings of other places not visited. Henri J. M. Nouwen wrote of this book: "For the countless people who search for a safe place in which they can confront the compulsions and obsessions of this world and claim the truth that they are the beloved sons and daughters of God, this book is a true treasure."

Regalbuto, Robert J. *A Guide to Monastic Guest Houses.* 3rd ed. Harrisburg, Pa.: Morehouse Publishing Company, 1998.

This book offers detailed information on accommodations in every state across America and in each Canadian province. Every place listed includes a description and history of the site, directions, costs, and maps.

Retreats Online (http://www.retreatsonline.com)

This two-year-old Vancouver based website provides basic information on retreats and retreat facilities worldwide. The designers include guidance on spiritual, business, health, artistic, and other retreats. It is a growing and easy-to-use resource.

NOTES

Chapter 1. A Church with Soul

1. For more information on bringing the gifts of the contemplative life to children and youth see Mark Yaconelli, "Youth Ministry: A Contemplative Approach," *The Christian Century* 116, no. 13 (April 21-28, 1999), 450-54.

Chapter 2. Becoming Contemplative

1. Dom Cuthbert Butler, *Western Mysticism: The Teachings of SS Augustine, Gregory, and Bernard on Contemplation and the Contemplative Life* (London: Constable & Company, Ltd., 1922), 47.

2. Paul Wilkes, *Beyond the Walls: Monastic Wisdom for Everyday Life* (New York: Doubleday, 1999), 179.

3. Thich Nhat Hanh, *Living Buddha, Living Christ* (New York: Riverhead Books, 1995), 60.

4. Thomas Keating, *Open Mind, Open Heart: The Contemplative Dimension of the Gospel* (Warwick, N.Y.: Amity House, Inc., 1986), 25.

5. Wilkes, *Beyond the Walls*, 179.

6. Richard J. Foster, *Streams of Living Water: Celebrating the Great Tradi-tions of Christian Faith* (San Francisco: Harper Collins Publisher, 1998), 5.

7. Wilkes, *Beyond the Walls*, 121.

8. Rueben P. Job, *Spiritual Life in the Congregation: A Guide for Retreats* (Nashville: Upper Room Books, 1997), 28.

9. Thich Nhat Hanh, *Living Buddha, Living Christ*, 26-27.

10. Phil Jackson and Hugh Delehanty, *Sacred Hoops: Spiritual Lessons of a Hardwood Warrior* (New York: Hyperion, 1995), 119.

11. John O'Donohue, *Anam Cara: A Book of Celtic Wisdom* (New York: Cliff Street Books, 1997), 71.

12. Thich Nhat Hanh, *Living Buddha, Living Christ*, 23.

Chapter 3. Shaping a Contemplative Retreat

1. Belden C. Lane, *The Solace of Fierce Landscapes: Exploring Desert and Mountain Spirituality* (New York: Oxford University Press, 1998), 64.

2. Sandra Cronk, *Dark Night Journey: Inward Re-patterning Toward a Life Centered in God* (Willingford, Pa.: Pendle Hill Publications, 1991), 22.

3. Ibid.

4. Lane, *The Solace of Fierce Landscapes*, 66-67.

5. Roger Housden, *Retreat: Time Apart for Silence and Solitude* (San Francisco: HarperSanFrancisco, 1995), 89.

6. Ibid., 89-90.

7. Ramona Miller, "Sacred Place: An Opening to the Inner Journey," *Presence* 5, no. 2 (May 1999), 9.

8. Cronk, *Dark Night Journey*, 30.

9. Lane, *The Solace of Fierce Landscapes*, 75.

Chapter 4. Leading a Contemplative Retreat

1. John Heider, *The Tao of Leadership: Lao Tzu's "Tao Te Ching" Adapted for a New Age* (Atlanta, Ga.: Humanics New Age, 1997), 53.

2. For a complete discussion of the role of the compassionate observer in the formation of spiritual directors see Jane E. Vennard, "The Compassionate Observer: An Experiential Model for Formation," *Presence* 4, no. 3 (1998), 24-33.

3. Heider, *The Tao of Leadership*, 13.

4. David A. Cooper, *Silence, Simplicity and Solitude: A Complete Guide to Spiritual Retreat* (Woodstock, Vt.: Skylight Paths Publishing, 1999), 131.

5. Heider, *The Tao of Leadership*, 23.

6. Ibid., 27.

7. Jack Kornfield, *A Path With Heart: A Guide through the Perils and Promises of Spiritual Life* (New York: Bantam Books, 1993), 222.

Chapter 5. Modified Monastic Scheduling

1. When I design a retreat, I begin with the schedule. Some people prefer to begin with the theme and the activities. If you are in the latter group, you might wish to read chapter 6 first and then return to chapter 5.

2. Some books on the integration of work and spirituality are: Jay A. Conger & Associates, *Spirit at Work: Discovering the Spirituality in Leadership* (San Francisco: Jossey-Bass Publishers, 1994); Matthew Fox, *The Reinvention of Work: A New Vision of Livelihood for Our Times* (San Francisco: Harper-SanFrancisco, 1994); Jeffrey K. Salkin, *Being God's Partner: How to Find the Hidden Link Between Spirituality and Your Work* (Woodstock, Vt.: Jewish Lights Publishing, 1994); and David Whyte, *The Heart Aroused: Poetry and the Preservation of the Soul in Corporate America* (New York: A Currency Book, 1994).

3. Wilkes, *Beyond the Walls*, 93.

4. Cooper, *Silence, Simplicity and Solitude*, 142.

5. Ibid., 88.

6. Wilkes, *Beyond the Walls*, 164.

7. See appendix B for suggested prayer and music resources to help in preparing worship and prayer services.

8. Lyn Klug, ed., *Soul Weavings: A Gathering of Women's Prayers* (Minneapolis: Augsburg Books, 1996), 114.

9. David Steindl-Rast with Sharon Lebell, *Music of Silence: A Sacred Journey Through the Hours of the Days* (Berkeley, Calif.: Seastone, 1998), 16.

10. Wilkes, *Beyond the Walls*, p. 138.

11. Ibid., 2.

Chapter 6. Themes, Activities, and Reflections

1. Only once in the 15 years I have been leading guided meditations has a retreatant had trouble leaving the imagery. This is very unlikely to happen, but if it does, the retreatant will need extra personal attention to be guided back from the imaginary experience in which he or she lingers.

2. For a guide to the Buddhist tradition of walking meditation, see Thich Nhat Hanh, *A Guide to Walking Meditation*, translated by Jenny Hoang and Anh Huong (New Haven, Conn.: Eastern Press, 1985).

3. John O'Donohue, *Anam Cara: A Book of Celtic Wisdom* (New York: Cliff Street Books, 1997), 48.

4. See Thelma Hall, *Too Deep for Words: Rediscovering Lectio Divina* (New York: Paulist Press, 1988); M. Basil Pennington, *Lectio Divina: Renewing the Ancient Practice of Praying the Scriptures* (New York: Crossroad, 1998); and William H. Shannon, *Seeking the Face of God* (New York: Crossroad, 1988).

5. Thomas Keating, "The Classical Monastic Practice of Lectio Divina," *Contemplative Outreach News* 12, no. 2 (1998), 1.

6. Ibid.

7. Joseph D. Driskill, *Protestant Spiritual Exercises: Theology, History and Practice* (Harrisburg, Pa.: Morehouse Publishing, 1999), 92-97.

8. If the retreat leader is not trained in the art of spiritual direction, one of the other alternatives is advised.

9. See Rose Mary Dougherty, *Group Spiritual Direction: Community for Discernment* (New York: Paulist Press, 1995) for a complete discussion of group spiritual direction. I have added the compassionate observers to Dougherty's model.

10. Gerald G. May, *Addiction and Grace* (San Francisco: Harper & Row, 1988), vi, 31, 147, 149, 175-76.

Chapter 7. Fruits of Contemplation

1. Thomas Keating, *Open Mind, Open Heart*, 114.

2. David A. Cooper, *Silence, Simplicity and Solitude: A Complete Guide to Spiritual Retreat* (Woodstock, Vt.: Skylight Paths Publishing, 1999), 11.

3. Ibid., 74.

4. Ibid., 76.

Appendix A. Home Retreat Week

1. Sometimes retreatants want their participation in home retreat week to remain confidential. Sylvia always honored that request by asking the congregation to pray "for all those on retreat this week." Retreatants were asked to pray "for the others on retreat this week." She found that praying without names did not lessen the experience of community or the power of being held in prayer.

2. The model for group spiritual direction described in chapter 6, page 81, was used in this group supervision session.